LESSONS FROM THE FATHER

1 PROLOGUE

We all have Guides, Guardians and Teachers, who are workers in God's plane and their sole purpose is to be our care takers.

****A note to the reader, when the Guides speak of man, they are speaking to mankind. There is no differentiation between men and women, because all are equal in God's eyes. The goal is for everyone to develop the ability to come into alignment with these Devine Guides and find their way to their purpose as designated by God. ****

The guides want the seekers of God's truths to have a solid foundation of faith and truth so they can thrive in the coming years, or you will fall prey to the coming call for sacrifice for the greater good.

The lessons are about life and faith in order for the faithful to able to survive the coming chaos. New challenges are coming to each person

MAY THE SEEDS OF DECEIT BE BLOWN AWAY LIKE CHAFF FROM THE WHEAT

regardless of what they believe, where they live or their financial status.

A new level of faith will be required if you are to keep your salvation. Everything depends on what you do in 2015. Are you ready? Are you spiritually prepared, when the insanity of the world comes to your door? You can no longer just go with the flow!

Many people believe they are invincible and they don't need God. Without God you will be at the mercy of the world. We are living in days of religious fanaticism and terrorism and this will be the weapons that will come against people of faith. If you are to survive you will have to rise above the fray and follow the truth from your Creator. Religious leaders will fall like a line of dominoes when the powers of the world come after the church.

God, the Father of us all, will not honor a people that does not honor Him!

Only you can discern the truth...it is up to you to read and decide if this is written for you.

ONE LIFE....ONE LOVE...ETERNAL

2 INTRODUCTION

Know that the Lord is with you today. The love of God is yours. There is much work to do. You must start devoting a part of each day to start getting to know your Father. This is a calling of faith to all of God's children. If you are willing to listen, this is a call from God to come home.

There is a need and a void in people's lives. They are not satisfied with their life. Take me for example, for me there is no other life, God is my center and my life….eternally, but it took me years to find my center and my purpose. You see I have always been a servant of God, I came here for a purpose but I got lost and it was a long lonely battle to find myself and become who I was created to be. If you have lost your way, then please take some time and let this help you find your center and find your real life, not a life of lies and illusion.

I was lost before I found the Lord. I had feelings of emptiness that nothing filled. I didn't know what was missing but I knew there had to be more than what I was living. I don't see how agnostics and atheists do it because, if this is all there is, if

MAY THE SEEDS OF DECEIT BE BLOWN AWAY LIKE CHAFF FROM THE WHEAT

all we are is a collection of accidental atoms that came together, then I do not see the point.

I had a near death experience at 21; I was blessed with surviving and coming back with knowledge that there was more than this life. You would think that I would have come back and started telling the world my experience, but I was riddled with guilt, struggling to rationalize who I was with what I saw. After the life I had led, who would listen to me? An actual Heaven, with Angels and Jesus just blew my mind. You see, I was one of those "spiritual" people that didn't believe in Heaven or in Hell, so when I wound up in Heaven that blew my new age theories out of the water.

So here I am 40 years later trying to do what God wants me to do and relay what God tells me that the world needs to know. This book is for anyone seeking answers and the truth. No one can tell you what is the truth, all I can do is relate what God has told me and you will have to listen to your heart to decide for yourself. Too many people take what some big time leader teaches and assumes it is the truth of the Creator. Time is running short and the clock is ticking. I must get this information into as many hands as possible

ONE LIFE...ONE LOVE...ETERNAL

MAY THE SEEDS OF DECEIT BE BLOWN AWAY LIKE CHAFF FROM THE WHEAT

because you are about to be tested and if you fail the test, well it's not going to be good.

Scientists once believed the Earth was flat, why because the only believed in what they could see. There is much more to the Universe than what you can see. You are more than you can imagine. You are created as a thumbprint of God.

People are so consumed by what they see and controlled by their emotions that they limit themselves. We have the power to create, to heal and to change our world. All that you are is not just the routine of life, the distractions and the lies of the world are holding God's children hostage and if you want to break free, there is a way. There is a path laid out before you, the challenge is finding the path and learning to find your way. This is what God has told me to relay to the world. So you see, if you feel the world has lost its mind, that's because it has. If you want to break away from the madness of the world, then come with me and let's see what God has in store for you.

ONE LIFE...ONE LOVE...ETERNAL

3 WHO WE ARE, WHAT WE ARE AND WHO'S TO BLAME.

People have been deceived into believing that they are products of their DNA and how they were raised. Don't lie to yourself and say you have no control on who you are, because you are the product of your upbringing! If you have no spiritual background, does that mean you can't connect with your spiritual higher-self? If both of your parents were alcoholics, does that mean you have to follow that path?

Genetics make you susceptible but they do not control you. You have the power to change these things, if you choose to use it. You need to realize what you can do and who you are because there is trouble ahead and you are going to need every ounce of your strength and ability to stay the course.

If you aren't grounded in faith and believing, then there is going to challenges put before you that you will not be able to handle. You will follow the wrong leader and find yourself in the wrong circumstances. There is a movement of very rich and powerful people who are manipulating the world's economy to their vision. They want to

MAY THE SEEDS OF DECEIT BE BLOWN AWAY LIKE CHAFF FROM THE WHEAT

take God out of our homes, our country and our lives.

It shouldn't be that hard to do since most people are so wrapped up in money, success and their toys that there is no time to focus on their spiritual existence. You might say you don't need all that God stuff in your life, but when all Hell breaks out on Earth, you just might change your mind. If you don't know God, then how will you recognize the Devil when he shows up at your door?

I hate to break it to you, but Lucifer is real. When he shows up, he makes it all sound so easy. He is beautiful to the eye and he says all the right things, because he is the great deceiver of mankind. This world is his playground and he is really busy. Man is being seduced into a world without hope. If there is no Satan then there is no God, if there is no God then there is no guidance, no grace and no life after death. If you are to win the battle, you have to understand there are forces at work that want to control you and keep you from the word of God.

Take a good look at what's going on in the world around you. We are inundated with movies and games where Lucifer and his evil are all powerful

MAY THE SEEDS OF DECEIT BE BLOWN AWAY LIKE CHAFF FROM THE WHEAT

and man is powerless to stop it. This is the greatest lie there is. Man was given dominion over all things. You have the power to cast out evil from your life but how can you take dominion if you don't understand who you are and what you are up against!

> *John 33:3 (Jesus said) Call unto me, and I will answer and show you great and mighty things, of which you know not.*

It is hard to know what to say and how to say it so that it touches a heart. I pray each day that the Lord will speak to me and I attempt to surrender my will and set myself aside so that I may receive what God wants me to write. This is not my writing but it is what I receive from the Lord. God told me to put down exactly what I receive; I can't edit or change anything. There isn't really any order to what I receive so I have just titled them like chapters. I pray you find some benefit from this work.

ONE LIFE...ONE LOVE...ETERNAL

4 HOW I GOT HERE.

How do I know there is a need and a void in people's lives? I was there, lost, empty and crying out for help. Nothing satisfied me, nothing brought me contentment and I was lost in the darkness and I couldn't find a way out. I remember crying out to God to help me, I knew I was more than what I saw in myself but I didn't know where to turn. The evangelists said all I had to do was ask and I would be saved and I would have a new life.

It was 3 in the morning and I got down on my knees and I cried out to God. I didn't hear Angels singing, I didn't feel any different at all! I had to wrestle with Satan to remove his hold on me. I had to struggle to eliminate the hold that had been on my family for generations. I was like Jacob wrestling the Angel for his blessing. Satan was not going to get out of my life without a fight!

I didn't know anything about God or generational curses that are passed down through the ages. There was a bond that was made with Satan decades before my birth that dedicated all following generations to be His. If you have never been taught, how do you know what to do? It

MAY THE SEEDS OF DECEIT BE BLOWN AWAY LIKE CHAFF FROM THE WHEAT

took me about 30 years to clear up my spirit because I didn't know who to turn to or what I needed to do. It's a miracle that I didn't wind up in some cult, because I was so desperate for something I knew was missing deep down within. God might have given me my life back, but I was so lost, I didn't know what to do or how to do it. I had a calling, I was just so bound up in condemnation and darkness that I didn't think anyone would listen to me! The thing of it is, that God chooses the least to do the most, so you will know it is God.

The last time I was truly attacked was 3 years ago. I was working so hard to clear up the final chains that were holding me back so I could truly receive the Holy Spirit and become whole at last. I had been fasting and praying for 10 days and on the night I broke my fast, I was alone in my bedroom praying. Out of the blue, I was riddled with anxiety, hands shaking and crying. My head was filled with doubts and Satan spoke to me (in my mind), telling me I was cursed, that I was promised to Him and He would never let go. I was an abomination to the Lord and that God didn't want me! All that I would do would fail and

MAY THE SEEDS OF DECEIT BE BLOWN AWAY LIKE CHAFF FROM THE WHEAT

people would think I was insane if I wrote down what God show's me!

I cried out to God for help, I asked for Christ to clear this out once and for all and to tell me the truth. I was crying and praying for what I thought was hours because time seemed to stand still. All of a sudden I was filled with a sense of peace and love. The attack was over and I was finally free!

A few nights later, I awoke at 3AM and standing at the foot of my bed was a very tall Angel. He was just standing there smiling, I was not afraid but as soon as I understood who he was, he was gone! I was wide awake and trying to understand what this meant. Suddenly I hear, this is my child and she is finally free! I feel tears of joy streaming down my face because I understood that I had made my way through the darkness.

There are many chains Satan uses to control us. Pornography, alcohol, drugs, fear, anxiety attacks and depression are just a few of the chains of the enemy. You will have to make the choice to follow the narrow path of God or just go on in the world the same old way. You must be patient and stay dedicated. You don't have to decide right now, just keep an open mind and remember God is with you every step of the journey, even if you

MAY THE SEEDS OF DECEIT BE BLOWN AWAY LIKE CHAFF FROM THE WHEAT

can't see or feel Him. You are loved. No one is beyond redemption, each new day is a new chance to grow and change.

So here we go, these are the writings... May the Lord bless you with revelation and understanding of the work and the purpose of the work, which is to lead you where you were created to be!

ONE LIFE...ONE LOVE...ETERNAL

5 THE WALK TO THE THRONE

The Lord is with you today. Each being will arrive in God's realm to face the Book of Life. You must make the walk to the Throne of God, and it will be paved with all the love you have given during your stay on this Earth. When you stand face to face with our Lord, how glorious will your walk be? What will you have created? What will the Lord see recorded in that Holy Book when you stand before the works of your life?

Understand that you are building your next life right here and now. Regardless of your choice you have one life eternal. There is no death; you transcend this life into your true self in God. What life do you want to live through eternity?

What you do now must be done as if the Savior were physically there with you, for you know that He is with you always…Keep in mind you **never** walk alone. You have Guardians, Guides and Teachers; Angels of God that have dedicated their existence to being there for you.

You are the creation of the Almighty; a product of God's love. You are made to be a product of love, a part of the Law of the Eternal one, made to be God on Earth. The Son of God came and walked

MAY THE SEEDS OF DECEIT BE BLOWN AWAY LIKE CHAFF FROM THE WHEAT

this Earth; all He did was done to show you how to live. All His suffering was endured so that you could be shown the possibility of what YOU can do.

You <u>MUST</u> face the fact that you are eternal, whether you live within God's love or you turn your back on his love. Imagine standing before the throne, in the presence of the Almighty, experiencing absolute love and being cast away, shunned from the Light, and being cast into isolation. Imagine the hurt He will experience from the disappointment he will feel in you. To see Him look at you and see a tear roll down in his cheek as he must put you aside. You MUST face the fact that you are eternal, whether you live with God or you shun his love. What if every day, throughout eternity, you live seeing others living on in bliss while you exist in the torment of separation

Do not live your life as a leper that cannot touch or live with those who are alive. Jesus healed the lepers, through faith in Him; to show those who live without faith are lepers in the Spirit. Healed they were rejoined with love and life so they could eat at the table of life and be shunned no more.

ONE LIFE...ONE LOVE...ETERNAL

MAY THE SEEDS OF DECEIT BE BLOWN AWAY LIKE CHAFF FROM THE WHEAT

One love, one life eternal, you create your life here and in eternity with your words, your attitude, your thoughts and your actions. The Holy Spirit is waiting for all who will be cleansed and offers their love to God and see Gods promise in all things.

ALL YOU DO IS RECORDED. YOU WRITE YOUR OWN BOOK…YOU CHOOSE.

ONE LIFE…ONE LOVE…ETERNAL

6 THE GOD SPARK

The Lord is with each of you. To love God is your purpose above all else. To commune with God is to complete the person. Most people are living a singular life of the ego. All they believe is what they see. All they seek is what they believe. Know this, you are a spiritual being. The atoms that compose you are a robe wrapped around your spirit.

When you seek God in prayer and meditation you are altering the vibration field of the atomic structure of the body. The touch of the Holy Spirit is the force that harmonizes the two bodies (spirit and physical) and brings them together. This is when your God spark becomes ignited and you become more of a spiritual being. When you become filled and unified; this is when you become born again! Being born again is the physical manifestation of being a spiritual being. This is a basic spiritual principal that eludes those on this spiritual plane of existence.

Just as you feed your physical body, you must feed the spiritual body. This comes with many

MAY THE SEEDS OF DECEIT BE BLOWN AWAY LIKE CHAFF FROM THE WHEAT

responsibilities. Prayer sends your communication to God and starts a chain reaction and throughout Heaven. All who love you and are connected with you also hear your prayer.

Meditation calms the mind and allows God's touch to be felt. Do not be afraid of the silence. Look up in your mind and allows God's touch to be felt. There is a peace in that touch that goes beyond explaining. Everything slows, the world becomes the illusion, and the spirit becomes the reality.

Negative emotions cannot survive the touch of God's presence. God is made of love, compassion and peace. You are an immortal being. To tell yourself that your life consists of only the here and now or that life does not survive death is an illusion created to eliminate the need for morality and justice.

If there is no God, if there is no continuance of life then why do we need to worry about living a good life? There will be no need for fairness and justice. Without God there is nothing to live for. The soul inhabits the body and upon death the soul returns to God's realm. You are here for such a small amount of time. There is no time to waste!

ONE LIFE...ONE LOVE...ETERNAL

7 CHANGING YOUR PERSPECTIVE

> **THE LORD IS ASKING YOU TO PUT ASIDE YOUR LIFE, YOUR WORLD AND WHAT YOU DESIRE FOR JUST A FEW MINUTES A DAY. CAN YOU DO THAT? CAN YOU DEVOTE A FEW MINUTES TO COMPLETELY DEDICATE YOUR MIND TO CHRIST AND THE HOLY SPIRIT?**

The Lord is with you today. The Lord God is pleased with the work of the daughter. Prayer and meditation bring forth the touch of the Holy Spirit.

Be filled with the power of the love of God. Let it fill every cell and let the body be healed and brought into alignment. Today is forever if you live in the moment. There is no turning of each moment, the clock is an illusion created by man. There is time for everything, because the moment is eternal. The moment is now!

When you are unhappy you feel it is forever and time does not pass. When you are happy you see

MAY THE SEEDS OF DECEIT BE BLOWN AWAY LIKE CHAFF FROM THE WHEAT

time is flying. Have you ever been engrossed in a project you love and it took hours of labor to accomplish it but it seemed like it only took a moment? This is because you exist in that moment, in that task.

Learn today that time is an illusion. Eat when you are hungry. Sleep when you are tired. Learn today not to be programmed by the clock. Conform for work and for scheduled events but learn to listen to your body, your heart and the lead of the Holy Spirit!

This is why we say there is a way to do all things. The moment is eternal; the self-imposed deadline is an illusion. All things will be done; all you need is to make an effort to be organized. Plan and prioritize yourself and your day.

Make God time your first priority, then plan what you need to do. See it all falling into place and going perfectly. Your day is like a river. It will flow between the banks unless you allow the rain to fall and cause the flood. You control your life, because you are an individual, one unit and you control what affects you. If a stranger comes up to you and starts screaming at you about their problems, how will that affect you? You didn't cause it and you can't fix it!

ONE LIFE...ONE LOVE...ETERNAL

MAY THE SEEDS OF DECEIT BE BLOWN AWAY LIKE CHAFF FROM THE WHEAT

You are an island. The winds will blow and the tide might rise but the island sits and waits for the calm. Be an island of calm in the storm. Control the emotions; do not be controlled by mere hormones! Stay God centered and the storms will become fewer and fewer. You attract what you are! What do you want to attract in your life?

Meditation will help you build your God center and give you the peace that you need to carry. Learn to be the eye of the storm. The world rages all around but the center is calm.

Control comes with the calm! Find your center and find the peace God sends you. I love you as always.

ONE LIFE...ONE LOVE...ETERNAL

MAY THE SEEDS OF DECEIT BE BLOWN AWAY LIKE CHAFF FROM THE WHEAT

8 INTENTIONAL Living

The Lord is with you today. Today is a day for being aware of why you do the things you do. We operate automatically most of our day. The things we do are done out of habit. Begin to try to have moments of intention.

Intention directs the mind and the flow of your day. Start the morning in prayer and communion with the Father of us all. Plan your day. What you intend to accomplish today?

Do not let the world rule your day. Put aside the irritations and negativity. You can accomplish whatever you focus on. The mind must be trained or it will run like a wild animal. Keep your mind on God in your work. God has you on His mind. Be an inspiration to others. Let the light shine through!

Don't sleep through your life. Focus on what you are doing, what you are thinking and why. Being aware and keeping your focus is a difficult habit to build. You are building a life of miracles. If you are unaware, you will not see God's work around you.

Intention allows the Holy Spirit to help guide you to your goals for the day. Seek the presence and guidance of the Holy Spirit today and be at peace.

ONE LIFE...ONE LOVE...ETERNAL

MAY THE SEEDS OF DECEIT BE BLOWN AWAY LIKE CHAFF FROM THE WHEAT

ONE LIFE...ONE LOVE...ETERNAL

9 DISTRACTIONS

The Lord is with you today. There are many things that distract the average person. Television, their phones, their jobs, etc. The list is very long. What we are asking here is that you give 10% of your time to God. You need to tithe your time to God. Would that be so very much to give? If you sleep 8 hours, that leaves you 16 hours in your day. That's about 90 minutes for you to strive to commune with God.

For instance if you would spend 30 minutes in the morning in prayer, praise and meditation before you break your nightly fast, you would only have 60 minutes to fit into your day. Take little God breaks during your day to talk to God. This will bring you back into focus on what is really important. If you find yourself lost in past mistakes or guilt, pull yourself back into the present with a little prayer for you to be able to release the past and move on. 5 minutes with God can take you from turmoil and distraction and bring you back into focus.

If things are going badly turn to God. If things are going really well, take 5 minutes to thank God. Gratitude breaks can take you to a new level of

MAY THE SEEDS OF DECEIT BE BLOWN AWAY LIKE CHAFF FROM THE WHEAT

consciousness. Even if you feel unhappy and frustrated, give God praise for your life and say you know this is not forever. God has you, if you will allow. You see, the enemy of man can't touch you while you are in God.

God can fix it all. God can cure all. You just have to give it time. When the enemy is attacking you, whether it is from illness or through someone who is trying to damage you or your reputation, if you will stay in God, you will get justice, you will get what you need.

When you are in alignment with God, when you are filled with love and gratitude, you are covered by the Holy Spirit. Your love and gratitude brings down God's spirit. You must understand this is your gift from God.

The greatest gift you will ever have is God's love. If you want to feel God's presence you must reach out, much like a baby that holds out his arms to be picked up and held. That is what God wants, for you to love Him like a child loves its parents. Just reach up and touch the spirit of God. Each effort will draw you closer. The more you commune with God, the stronger His presence will come unto you. Peace and calm comes to those who strive to be in God's presence.

ONE LIFE...ONE LOVE...ETERNAL

MAY THE SEEDS OF DECEIT BE BLOWN AWAY LIKE CHAFF FROM THE WHEAT

It will take effort at first, but as you form the routine of reaching out to God and asking for His guidance and protection, you will begin to see a change in yourself. The change will come from within.

Dedicate yourself for 30 days and see if you don't have more peace and contentment in your life. Keep a short diary for 30 days. Comment on how you feel. Take note of what happens around you. Watch for change and be aware of your surroundings.

Making God part of your day makes God an active partner in your life. When you partner with Christ Jesus, you will never have to walk alone again! No matter the trials of the world, you will have Christ as your partner. Know that you will have trials, that is just the way the world is, but if you know you have Christ to get you through, you will have an easier walk and you will shorten the duration.

Much of the world's trials and tribulations are of man's own creation, there is a lack of contentment in their lives and they wind up chasing illusions, trying to find happiness. They are never satisfied with what they have. It seems no matter how great their blessing, they strive for

ONE LIFE...ONE LOVE...ETERNAL

MAY THE SEEDS OF DECEIT BE BLOWN AWAY LIKE CHAFF FROM THE WHEAT

more. If you appreciate what you have, if you live in gratitude, then God's blessings will flow.

If you are negative and angry all of the time, then you draw negative things into your life. Expect greater things! Be grateful for what you have. God's blessings are limitless! You are in control of your life and how you live it.

If you don't take the rudder of your ship you will never get to your destination.

God knows your purpose. God knows where you need to go. Sail your ship on calm waters and get safely to shore.

Be blessed and know God is with you.

ONE LIFE...ONE LOVE...ETERNAL

10 FEAR

The Lord is with you today. The lies of Satan are the voice in your mind at 3AM. The goal of the Enemy is to keep you locked in the past and the imagined danger of the future. If Satan keeps you in the bondage of the past, or worrying about the future, your present time will be wasted and you will be captured by fear.

Fear keeps you from manifesting your dreams. Fear is in the court of Satan and will strike you like a knife in the heart. Now is the time to begin living. It is time to take the doubt, guilt and regret to Christ and allow the Grace of God to wash you clean. You are forgiven the second you present it to Christ Jesus, but you must forgive yourself and release the past. Christ comes to you each day with the sunrise ready to lead you into a new day. Yesterday was like the morning mist that burns away with the coming of the Sun. To fear the new day is to doubt Christ. Allow the love of Father of us all to wash away the doubt and fill you with the peace and knowledge that Christ will lead and protect you, if only you would allow it.

Trust in the Lord and face the new challenges of your new life that is prepared for you. Life is your

MAY THE SEEDS OF DECEIT BE BLOWN AWAY LIKE CHAFF FROM THE WHEAT

training ground. Everything that happens is for a purpose. Everything you endure is preparing you for your future. There is a reason you are here. There is work to be done. How can you do the work that lies ahead if you are not prepared? When you get to the Throne and face the Akashic record, you will have to face your life, what will you say in your defense? How can you plead you're your case with ignorance?

You are now warned, you will have to face your life. What would you rather fear your life on Earth or eternity? You have a choice, you have free will and you have the ability to see what the truth is and what the lies of the common man are. The common man lives for his paycheck and his possessions.

The uncommon man sees the world for what it truly is and he does the best to live a life of truth and love. Follow the narrow path of Light until the time you can join the Father of us all. Fear, hate, distrust and anger are the tools of Satan to control you. Peace, joy and love are the gifts of a life in the light.

The choice lies before each of us!

ONE LIFE...ONE LOVE...ETERNAL

11 COMING CHALLENGES

The Lord is with you today. Know that you are loved. There is a great challenge coming before all of you. You will be tested and only the faithful shall come to truly know God. Many are called into service. They say the words, but their heart and mind are weak. That is why you must know God. If you think you believe or if you hope there is a God and he has a purpose for you, then you will fail.

Your faith must be built on a foundation of bedrock. Nothing can come from the world that can change your heart. Your inner Temple must be built on faith and on belief. The time for questioning God's will and purpose has passed. You must be like water, flowing with immense power, but to the eye you seem peaceful and serene.

Your Temple is the body of Christ that grows within; the Temple of the spirit man that is fed by God's Holy Spirit. Most churches today do not want you to know the Holy Spirit. They want you to believe that all you have to do is utter a sentence and the kingdom of God is yours. The Kingdom is there for those beings that have

MAY THE SEEDS OF DECEIT BE BLOWN AWAY LIKE CHAFF FROM THE WHEAT

assumed the mantle of Christ. No, not the second coming, but the spirit of the holy one... The Christ!

To truly understand and see this you will have to receive Revelation that only comes through true connection, alignment and communion with the Holy Spirit. You must work for this. Meditation, prayer of petition and a deep desire is required for you to see the kingdom of God. There is a heaven, but also there is the kingdom; salvation gets you to heaven but the kingdom is for those who were warriors in God's spiritual Army.

Men of God are seekers and warriors. They are separated from the masses of the world by choice. Do not make this choice lightly. This is a covenant with God! Study this book and research the word of God for revelation to see the truth. To win this battle for your soul, we must enter through the heart to convince the mind. Open hearts and minds is all that are required to build your Temple!

The words of God are not there for debate. The words of God are intended to teach and to lead. The words are only words unless they fall upon an open heart that is seeking the truth.

ONE LIFE...ONE LOVE...ETERNAL

MAY THE SEEDS OF DECEIT BE BLOWN AWAY LIKE CHAFF FROM THE WHEAT

Pray each day for an open heart and receive his love and revelation. If you do not believe in miracles get ready, because once you become anointed, miracles will follow. Not all will see this Revelation; not all will follow this path. What will you choose? What will you do? God is calling you!

Study the works of God in his books in the Bible, study the direction this book will take you, and you will find that always say is backed up in his book the Bible. Christ is given us the instructions, the way, and has sacrificed so that we might see it's up to us if we follow. Guard your heart and your mind and follow God's way.

> *Isaiah 58:11 and the Lord shall guide you continually, satisfy your soul in drought and make fat thy bones. You shall be like a watered garden and like a spring of water, whose waters fails not.*

ONE LIFE....ONE LOVE....ETERNAL

MAY THE SEEDS OF DECEIT BE BLOWN AWAY LIKE CHAFF FROM THE WHEAT

12 THE STATE OF THE WORLD

Men of the world are working to create a one world government and the religious church works for a one world church, both will not be God based. You should have no fear and work in the peace of the Lord for he has seen all this and knows the performance before the curtain rises.

God sees the ministrations of man before they even designed to work their plans. The enemy has people blinded into believing there is no God to guide and protect them. There is strength that comes from faith and it is through our relationship we will have the unending guidance of our Father. You see it takes great strength, to stand for God, while we love our enemies and lead them through our actions.

The answer lies within for those that submit to God, and put their plans and will aside and follow God. Only that way will we see the victory for this world. There is a greater plan than that of man and we cannot understand this as mere humans. The meek shall inherit the earth and the kingdom of God awaits those who submit their will and become obedient to God.

ONE LIFE...ONE LOVE...ETERNAL

MAY THE SEEDS OF DECEIT BE BLOWN AWAY LIKE CHAFF FROM THE WHEAT

In the peace of God there lies the guidance and the way. A war is coming! They are gathering and planning to wipe out the believers. But the good news is a brotherhood will be formed to fight for Christ. For God to be on our side and we must put aside pagan influences and have a true heart and pure worship of the Father. The Lord is calling forth His children to band together for the coming of people.

The love and purpose of Christ cannot be understood or imagined. We need to be filled with the fullness of God, so we may have the vision and the understanding to follow. You are able to do above your knowing abundantly, according to the power that works in us for His glory and will. He gives us whatever we need to do His works, so walk with confidence and know you are worthy of the vocation that you are called to do.

There is one body, one spirit and you are called for a purpose and that is to do the works of God, but you must work to keep the unity of the spirit in order to maintain your inspiration and continue to follow the will of God. You must keep your daily devotional.

You must keep the Holy Spirit as your first priority so you do not start to put yourself first and begin

MAY THE SEEDS OF DECEIT BE BLOWN AWAY LIKE CHAFF FROM THE WHEAT

to follow what your mind tells you, you should do. Your mind will attempt to lead you astray! When I began the actual writing of this book, I thought I would follow the direction from the Father and then I would get on with my regular life. The more I studied, prayed and meditated the more the vocation became a part of me that I cannot leave behind. This is now my life!

There is a commandment to each and every one of us that strives to do His works, you must make it a part of your heart and give the glory of your work to God in His name. Your work will become your life, just as your passion for Him will grow. As you pray, meditate and focus on God and his word, you will be planting a seed that will grow just as the mustard seed that the Bible speaks of grows into a mighty tree. This is a metaphor for how the smallest seed, the smallest spark of God, can grow into a mighty warrior.

Your works must follow the mandates of God or it is not of God. If your works are to teach the truth and follow the walk of Christ, then the blessings and the abundance of God will be yours. You see man's life is not meant to be a life of poverty. The Lord wants His children to prosper but just seeking abundance is not to be your goal. You

MAY THE SEEDS OF DECEIT BE BLOWN AWAY LIKE CHAFF FROM THE WHEAT

must not allow things to be your focus because your purpose should be God and God will provide for you. You must do your work as a partner with God and you must be productive. The tree that does not produce fruit will be killed from the roots up.

If you have worked and failed, it was not a punishment but it was part of your education. I tried so many times to build a business that would help people change their lives and see what they were doing to themselves. I always failed, but I as a person grew from what I learned from the effort. God was training me for this work. The fact it took me 20 years to realize my purpose was because I didn't know how to move closer to God and commune with him. Only through the Holy Spirit did I come to my purpose. I don't want it to take you 20 years. That's why I write. You must keep your eyes focused on the goal, because the eyes are the window to the spirit. All you experiences fed to the mind through the eyes and the ears. That is why you need to pray out loud and speak what you wish to attain.

You must be steadfast in all your works. If you must walk alone, then you must be willing. Most times that is a test of your strength, faith and true

MAY THE SEEDS OF DECEIT BE BLOWN AWAY LIKE CHAFF FROM THE WHEAT

purpose. Once the people who love you see your passion and determination they will slowly begin to accept the change and your work. You must show God what you feel. Express to God your love. Give him the glory for your life. You must accept your inheritance as a child of God. You are of Royal blood; claim your inheritance on earth from the Father, because it and is already created in Heaven waiting for you.

> **_Revelations 22:12   and behold, I come quickly: and my reward is with me, to give every man according to his works_**

The Lord will come into your life if you seek his will, follow his word and seek his voice. Just as the Lord's Prayer states, thy will be done on earth as it is in heaven! Everything we need is known before we even realize it or know it, just waiting for us to call it down into being. Everyone in heaven lives for the will of God and we must strive to worship and work on earth with the same heart and obedience. We may not be perfect; we may fall down, but know that regardless of how far you fall each moment is a chance for a new beginning. God knows were not perfect, he knows were only

MAY THE SEEDS OF DECEIT BE BLOWN AWAY LIKE CHAFF FROM THE WHEAT

human but he expects us to keep trying. He expects us to get up, brush off the dirt and get back to what we know we should be doing. Each moment we face a choice and each moment is a chance to start over.

What greater task could you have than to do the works of God? What greater reward is there than to have his favor and his love. God takes care of his children and he welcomes home the rebellious and forgives us. It is to the faithful the Lord rewards with his love, favor and abundance. Know this, as you give to the world, so shall you receive!

Millions of people believe they are spiritual but they say they do not follow Christ. They understanding playing with the metaphysics of God's power but they have eliminated the divinity of Jesus. The new age philosophy uses the principles of the spoken word and visualization to guide their attempt to steer their life. They use the natural power of God which he gave to all his children, but they do not give Him praise, glory, and the worship that is required to capture the love and attention of the Lord. We cannot eliminate Jesus's Divinity and reduce God to a mere spiritual science.

ONE LIFE...ONE LOVE...ETERNAL

MAY THE SEEDS OF DECEIT BE BLOWN AWAY LIKE CHAFF FROM THE WHEAT

The deceiver's will use any means to lead mankind from worship and the glory to the one who made it possible for them to have these abilities. They do not seek the will, the voice of God, or use his word for guidance. To live in favor we must: seek His will and His voice and read His word for guidance and Revelation. We need to be faithful, obedient and listen to the voice of God. You yearn for the love of the Father, add these things to your life and you will build a full complete life and there will be no question as to your purpose. I want you to know the God loves you today as he does each and every day he just wants you to be the best that you can be and fulfill the potential that he built into you so that you have the ability to fulfill your purpose.

ONE LIFE...ONE LOVE...ETERNAL

13 TO BE CHRISTIAN

The Lord is with you today. To be loved is the greatest gift of God to his children. More and more people are seeking a better way to live their lives. Men of God are seeking a meaning for all the turmoil in the world! The lies within the egos of man have run rampant through religion like a virus and his breeding self-righteousness and condemnation.

To live a life for God you must put aside your judgment and hate. You think it is just a matter of believing in Christ to succeed. Christ came to teach and died to open the veil and allow all who seek to commune with the Father of us all. Christ taught us about healing, love and forgiveness. These are the essential things that are required of you.

We as followers of the message cannot allow our egos to put ourselves above others. The blessed of God should feel compassion for the lost, the poor and the ignorant. Christ himself came to be a servant and how can we put ourselves in a position above his?

To you it is simple to love God, but the enemy has the lost in bondage because they believe the lies

MAY THE SEEDS OF DECEIT BE BLOWN AWAY LIKE CHAFF FROM THE WHEAT

to such a degree that they cannot see the truth. God can forgive all. Be on your guard where the judgment of others is concerned because as you judge you too will be judged. Keep your heart open to the love of God. Always remember the teachings of Christ Jesus. Honor God with the works that you do.

ONE LIFE...ONE LOVE...ETERNAL

14 LAYING THE FOUNDATION

Your foundation is the basis of which you will build the faith that is required for you to accomplish your purpose. This is why you need it. You will receive what you need and you will see where you're going.

This is the truth about dogma, which separates man from God. Man has created the dogma of religion! Every time God sends a messenger, the message was lost in man's interpretations or man begins worshiping the messenger. Religion not worship is destroying the earth. Lines of separation are being drawn which feed hate and retribution and they are pulling us farther and farther from God.

This was true at the time of the Old Testament, so God decided that he would take a small part of himself and place it in the woman Mary, wrap it in flesh and send the world an example of how mankind was designed to operate in God's image. I know in my heart the God spoke the truth when he said you can do all things just as I have, and even more, if you believe.

We as men have lost our divinity and our purpose. We are so busy being entertained by the things of

MAY THE SEEDS OF DECEIT BE BLOWN AWAY LIKE CHAFF FROM THE WHEAT

this world and we're so proud of our technology, even though we have lost our spiritual self. It doesn't even seem to matter to most people that they have no spiritual life, they have no relationship with God and this is the saddest thing that God is ever seen! I want you to know that each day when we go on our merry way and we don't include God in all that we do, we grieve the Holy Spirit!

There are people who claim to be leaders, who claim they are showing you the way, but they have watered down the message to make it more palatable to people. They have even gone so far as to state that the teachings of Jesus are not relevant to this world, they want you to believe that all you have to do is declare out loud that Jesus as your Lord and Savior and you are saved, you operate under grace, for all time. Regardless of what you do, through one statement, you are saved! These people will fall like dominoes when the upheaval comes. They have placed themselves upon an altar, and they have deemed themselves an interpreter of the word of God. They have decided what can be eliminated, what is no longer relevant, so they can have their mega-churches and be idolized as a leader and a speaker for God,

MAY THE SEEDS OF DECEIT BE BLOWN AWAY LIKE CHAFF FROM THE WHEAT

when they are so many of them that are doing a disservice to people who may truly be seeking God.

They are causing people to build their mansions on sand! And when the wind blows and the tide rises their mansions will be washed away because they were not built on a foundation of truth, a foundation based on the true word of God and they will fall to the enemy when times get hard.

We were born with the power to manifest. We were created with the power to create what God has prepared for us. We need to learn to control this power and to do the will of God on earth. We are like children running around with no rules and no idea of what we are doing. You see the power is there regardless of whether you understand it or not. When you speak, you create, regardless of your intention. If you speak ill of anyone or anything you are calling that upon yourself. When you judge others for the way they live their lives, which are exactly how you will be judged. That is why you need to understand the laws the Lord has set down so you will understand what you are doing. God knows what you need, it is prepared for you and it is up to you to call it into being.

ONE LIFE...ONE LOVE...ETERNAL

MAY THE SEEDS OF DECEIT BE BLOWN AWAY LIKE CHAFF FROM THE WHEAT

The creator has a plan for you because you are special, one-of-a-kind and made for a purpose. You have been given special talents and abilities that are specific for your purpose. Only through our relationship and communion with the Holy Spirit can we truly understand our calling and change the things that be changed so that we can manifest the life that the Lord has planned for us. This is so essential to know, to understand and to accept. Unless you adopt this into your life you will never know the meaning and the purpose that you were created for. What if you walk away and say this is not for me, I am too busy, I'm too successful and I just don't have time for this and you were meant to lead someone that will be lost to the kingdom of God, because you were too busy?

Once you decide to accept God in your life, and you accept the Holy Spirit as your guide, and you accept Christ as your guiding spirit, then and only then will you begin to receive your gifts of the Holy Spirit. These gifts are there specifically for you so that you may learn to discern the truth and recognize those that seek to manipulate you and control you. God wants you to stand for something. God wants you to succeed and be the

ONE LIFE...ONE LOVE...ETERNAL

MAY THE SEEDS OF DECEIT BE BLOWN AWAY LIKE CHAFF FROM THE WHEAT

person that you were meant to be so that you may be prepared for the trials that lay before us in the coming times.

If you don't believe that there is an upheaval coming with trials and tribulations which will be laid at the door of every human being on this planet, then you will be unprepared. There is insanity and a bloodlust that cannot be stopped regardless of how much we pray or how much we ignore it. All is been prophesied in the Book of Revelations and if you watch it's like a checklist being fulfilled. These things are brought before you not to scare you but to prepare you. The enemy of man wants us to fail and God wants us to succeed. Which path will you follow? Each individual must make this choice!

> *Revelations 3:5 He that overcomes, the same shall be clothed in white raiment; I will not blot out his name out of the book of life, but I will confess his name before my Father and before His angels.*

He that stands fast in the Lord and overcomes this world will be clothed in the white robe of

ONE LIFE...ONE LOVE...ETERNAL

MAY THE SEEDS OF DECEIT BE BLOWN AWAY LIKE CHAFF FROM THE WHEAT

salvation, wear a golden belt of righteousness and upon it will hang the key to the Kingdom. In your hand you will carry a lantern that will shine with the Light of the Lord.

ONE LIFE...ONE LOVE...ETERNAL

15 THE CALLING

The Lord is with you today. Know that you are loved. There is a great challenge coming before all of you. You will be tested and only the faithful shall come to truly know God.

Many are called into service. They may respond and say the words but their hearts and their minds are weak. That is why you must know God. If you think you believe or if you hope there is a God and he has a purpose for you, then you will fail. Your faith must be built on a foundation of bedrock. Nothing can come from the world that can change your heart. Your church must be built on faith and on belief. The time for questioning God's will and purpose are passed. You must be like water, flowing with immense power, but to the eye you seem peaceful and serene.

Your temple is the body of Christ that grows within. A temple that houses a spirit man that is fed by God's Holy Spirit. The churches today do not want you to know the Holy Spirit. They want you to believe that all you have to do is utter a sentence and the kingdom of God is yours. The kingdom is there for those beings that have assumed the mantle of Christ! Know I'm not

MAY THE SEEDS OF DECEIT BE BLOWN AWAY LIKE CHAFF FROM THE WHEAT

speaking of the second coming, but the spirit of the Holy One... The Christ!

To truly understand and see this you will have to receive revelation that only comes through true connection, alignment and communion through the Holy Spirit. You must work for this. Meditation, prayer of petition and a deep desire is required for you to see. There is a heaven, but also there is the Kingdom. Salvation gets you to heaven but the Kingdom is for those who were warriors in God's spiritual Army.

Men of God are seekers and warriors! They are separated from the masses by choice. But I warn you, do not make this choice lightly. This is a covenant with God. Study the book and research the word of God for revelation to see the truth. To win the battle for your soul we must enter through the heart to convince the mind. Only through open hearts and minds can the Lord touch you because that's all that is required.

The words of God are not there for debate! The words of God are intended to teach and to heal, but the words are only words unless they fall upon an open heart that is seeking the truth. Pray each day for an open heart and receive his love and revelation. If you do not believe in miracles, get

MAY THE SEEDS OF DECEIT BE BLOWN AWAY LIKE CHAFF FROM THE WHEAT

ready, because once you become anointed the miracles will follow!

Not all will see and understand this revelation!

Not all will follow this path. What will you choose? What will you do? God is calling you.

ONE LIFE...ONE LOVE...ETERNAL

MAY THE SEEDS OF DECEIT BE BLOWN AWAY LIKE CHAFF FROM THE WHEAT

16 SPIRITUAL GROWTH

The Lord is with you today. This is a book about spiritual awakening and growth. You need to carry your heart like a precious jewel. The heart is the seat of your soul. Do not give your heart away to a liar and a false prophet. Discern who you will follow. Keep your eyes on God; listen for the inner voice to guide you, the Holy Spirit is there for you. The love of God is yours, be at peace in the Lord every day.

To the people the Lord sends his love. Know that there is a great change coming in the world. There will be many tests put before you. You do not have to make this walk alone. These messages are intended to help guide you and help you be prepared for what you will face in the future.

These lessons are sent out to you in a specific order so you may lay a foundation of knowledge and build upon it. You may be aware of parts of the message, but it is like painting a picture. You cannot paint in only one color, with one brush. You must learn to add light to the picture. The base must be prepared so that the canvas is ready to apply the paint so that the painting will last. The outline is laid out carefully, and then the

MAY THE SEEDS OF DECEIT BE BLOWN AWAY LIKE CHAFF FROM THE WHEAT

areas are filled in. That is what these instructions are intended to do. To take who you are and help you build a clear picture of God and the reality of the world for you.

There is much to learn. There are many revelations to come. Your being here is not an accident, you were guided here. This is an opportunity that must be decided by the heart and within the spirit. All that is done here is for you.

Open your heart and listen to the still soft voice that calls you into action. Do not go another day without feeding your soul and preparing for the challenges that are before you.

Be at peace in the Lord Christ Jesus. The love of God is yours, but you must choose your fate, your purpose and your destiny.

ONE LIFE...ONE LOVE...ETERNAL

17 LOVE Relationship

The Lord is with you today. There are so many people who have never been shown how to have a love relationship with God. They have been taught the premise of a vengeful God who wants to punish, but God is a loving Father who wants His children to be loved, happy and successful. All God asks of you is that you make God your first priority. Nothing should come between you and your creator!

There are people who say they love the Lord but everything comes first before God. Football, baseball, vacations, work, video games, partying, the list is endless! Anything you put before God is an Idol. God does not allow Idol worshipers to fall under His blessings. You must love the Lord your God in all that you do. You must honor God in the way you live, behave and speak. You must live as if God was at your side, because He is.

God wants a loving relationship with each and every child. God wants you to have the blessings He has prepared for you. To receive, you must show God your heart. Pray and give thanks. Praise God for who he is and what he means to you. Relationships must be built on one prayer at a

MAY THE SEEDS OF DECEIT BE BLOWN AWAY LIKE CHAFF FROM THE WHEAT

time. God hears your thoughts. God wants to hear your voice in prayer. Speak your prayer, speak your relationship, and speak what moves your heart.

Don't be a prisoner of the world! Find the missing part of your life; find the love that is unending and eternal.

Be at peace in the Lord. Walk under the covering of Christ Jesus' love.

<u>MAY THE SEEDS OF DECEIT BE BLOWN AWAY LIKE
CHAFF FROM THE WHEAT</u>

18 LOVE II

The love of God is the greatest gift to man. The Grace of God comes as a result of that love. Know that the Lord is with you today. Keep your heart on the message of love. Never doubt you are loved. Keep your mind on God throughout your day.

When you wander into the distraction of the world around you, if you will refocus on God, this will help you stay on your path. This will help you keep others from pulling you into their drama and their made up life.

People create most of the turmoil in their lives. They look for reasons to be upset and pull others into their world. You can perceive hurt and slight everywhere. When you analyze and criticize you are walking in judgment. That is the domain of the Lord. You call into your life what you judge against.

Do your best and allow others to find their own way. Be at peace in the Lord. The love of God is the greatest gift. The grace of God is the result of his love.

ONE LIFE...ONE LOVE...ETERNAL

19 OUR RESPONSIBILITY

The Lord is with you today to be loved is the greatest gift of God to his children. More and more people are seeking a better way to live their lives. Men of God are seeking a meaning for all the turmoil in the world.

The lies of man have run through all the religions like of a virus and his breeding self-righteousness and condemnation. To live a life for God, you must put aside judgment and hate. To you it just means believing in Christ. Christ came to teach and died to open the veil so that all who seek to communing with the Father of us all. Christ teaches healing, love and forgiveness.

We as followers of the message cannot allow ourselves to put ourselves above the others. The blessed of God should feel compassion for the lost, the poor and the ignorant. The lies of man blocked the people from believing. Superstitions, false idols analyze keep them in bondage and blinded by the lies, which are keeping them all blind to the light. They do not understand God's law. They think the law is the Torah or the 10 Commandments. These hold the rules on how to live and to guide you to God. The laws of God are

MAY THE SEEDS OF DECEIT BE BLOWN AWAY LIKE CHAFF FROM THE WHEAT

the science that we can work on earth. Man has dominion, so God works through man. Mankind has been given the power to use the power of God in their lives. We must create their intention. We must claim what is ours. God knows the needs and hasn't prepared for you. It is up to each person to focus on what they need.

Pray and commune, see what you need, see yourself with that in hand, and feel the emotion of when you receive and give thanks as if you have already received it. Keep praying until you feel the shift and you know you have broken through. Free will in dominion is a great responsibility and mankind is failing the world. God needs us to act with him for his will to be fulfilled on this world.

ONE LIFE...ONE LOVE...ETERNAL

<u>May the seeds of deceit be blown away like chaff from the wheat</u>

20 THE ENEMY OF MAN

But it is all known to all who will listen. Just as sure as there is a God in heaven, there exists the enemy of mankind. To believe there is only good in the world and all things spiritual are good is foolish. If all things were good, then why is the world on such a path of destruction? When mankind plays in God's realm without permission, you are operating outside of God's protection and you are leaving yourself open to all types of influences.

Men of God need this revelation: Satan used Judas Iscariot to betray Christ in an attempt to stop the influence of Christ on earth. Little did he know that he was allowing the prophecy of Christ to be fulfilled for all man to witness! The work of God has continued, even though the enemy has worked everything he could do against God's children.

<u>St. John 13:3   Supper being ended, the devil now having put into the heart of Judas Iscariot, Simon's son to betray him</u>

ONE LIFE...ONE LOVE...ETERNAL

MAY THE SEEDS OF DECEIT BE BLOWN AWAY LIKE CHAFF FROM THE WHEAT

Lucifer hates man because man is loved by God above all others. There was a jealousy that became hate. Satan wants to prove that God is wrong to love people that are so weak and so easily led astray.

God loves his children above all else and wants you to be prepared for all that comes before you. You were created at this specific time for a purpose. There are forces loose in the world that will try to stop you. They will put obstacles in your way; they will plant seeds of doubt in your mind and will try to make you doubt that you have a purpose. The stronger the assaults to stop you, the greater works you are destined for.

Know this, if you walk away from God you will leave the shelter and protection of the Lord and you will fall away from your purpose. Who will do your part if you leave? The world holds no joy for those who stand alone against the storm to come.

You will need the voice of God to show you the truth and to recognize when you are being led off the narrow path, God has put before you.

ONE LIFE....ONE LOVE...ETERNAL

21 THE ENEMY AT WORK

Love is the key to progress. Filling the spirit and the body in worship brings the spirit to a higher level of attunement. There is much work to be done. The love of God must be cast upon the ocean of man. Only through the love of God can the upheaval be survived. The destroyer of mankind comes in sheep's clothing, painting a picture of logic and reason that is based in destruction. He is the beginning of the upheaval to come.

Man judges by appearance, so he will be a comely looking person. His voice will mesmerize the people and they will follow like sheep. Be aware of those who ask for just a little sacrifice for the greater good. The lure of the lie will be great! Men are so easily deceived, because he does not seek the discernment of the Holy Spirit. The deceiver is so strong that only through the Holy Spirit can you see the truth.

That is why we have led you to grow in spirit. The connection of the spirit is so strong now through faith and prayer and focused meditation on the Lord that you have healed the mind and you have achieved a new evolution of the spirit self. You are

MAY THE SEEDS OF DECEIT BE BLOWN AWAY LIKE CHAFF FROM THE WHEAT

being led to accept the responsibility to be guardians and warriors in the battle for the spiritual survival of God's children.

Millions will accept a false Idol and leave the path of God. Even if you deny God and live a state of denial, that will be a false Idol that you have assumed. Anything that comes before God in your life is a false Idol! Any ideology that is not of the one true God is false.

You must listen to your heart and not to your mind. Do not be seduced by the mass media that will fall at his feet. Guard what you accept as truth, freedom given up cannot be taken back. It will be taken an inch at a time, in the name of unity and peace. Eventually your right to free assembly will be limited. Your right to defend your home and your family will be gone. Watch and be aware. The signs are there. The wheels are in motion. You will need your foundation of faith, you will need your shelter and you will need the guidance of the Holy Spirit. If you are prepared, you will survive and be a voice of the Lord in the world.

The love of the Lord is with his warriors. Be a watchman for the Lord in the world.

ONE LIFE...ONE LOVE...ETERNAL

MAY THE SEEDS OF DECEIT BE BLOWN AWAY LIKE CHAFF FROM THE WHEAT

22 MANIFESTING

The reason you will be taught the power of manifesting the Lord's work is so you can be prepared for the trials that are upon us. There will be an effort to strip us of all of our rights and to turn over all authority to the government. The bill of rights in the United States will be stripped away in the name of safety and equality. The government will offer us security, food and all the necessities but only to those who give allegiance to the powers that are in charge.

Learn about the tongue and the power of the voice. Learn how we can damage our spirit by what we do, by what we listen to and by what we watch. We will teach you about the emotions and how they are the third part of manifestation. Fear is the destroyer, the same way doubt destroys our work. If we let them keep us in fear, they will win. Only through faith and believing is there hope.

- These things are essential for you to understand.
- There is much work ahead for the seekers.
- They will be a foundation of change for the world.
- They will be the new age of believers.

ONE LIFE...ONE LOVE...ETERNAL

MAY THE SEEDS OF DECEIT BE BLOWN AWAY LIKE CHAFF FROM THE WHEAT

- They will be workers on earth for change.
- They will be the voice of God on earth fulfilling the will of God.
- You must lead them to the tree of life.
- You must show them the narrow path.
- You must allow them to begin their climb

Be at peace in the Lord knowing that he is always with you. This is that is why this is written for you.

ONE LIFE...ONE LOVE...ETERNAL

23 MANIFESTING II

The love of God is yours. There is a way for each individual to come to a higher level of connection with the guiding plan of God.

To love God is the first key. Build up the love relationship first. Make it your highest priority.

To praise God is the second key. God needs you to talk to Him, tell Him how you feel. This is the tool that calls forth the presence of God into your world. Call out to God; tell Him you need Him in your life. Tell the Lord you love Him! This is the main path; you must pray and give praise to build a relationship with your Father, your creator and the Lord of us all. There is a path, but to find it, you must have a guiding relationship.

The third key is meditation. Calming of the mind and the body allows you to receive. Just as prayer and praise call forth God's presence, meditation prepares you to receive. This is the step to balance and unity.

The fourth key is your emotions. Negative emotions destroy your connection and take over your life and call forth diseases such as cancer,

MAY THE SEEDS OF DECEIT BE BLOWN AWAY LIKE CHAFF FROM THE WHEAT

high blood pressure and depression. Negative emotions destroy all your creative powers and attract the same emotions from others.

Positive emotions such as happiness, joy and love feed the body and the mind. This is the emotion of creativity. If you want the power of creation so you may manifest God's will, you will have to stay positive and emotionally engaged for the process to work. This is the hardest step for most people. You must not allow the emotions of others to influence you. You are an island in the ocean of mankind.

To love God above all is essential!! You must be devoted to what you call into being. If there is no meditation or if prayer time is slighted you will not grow. Only you can pray it into being!

The fifth key is the power of the tongue. The voice brings forth what you want or what you don't want. That is why it is called the double edged sword that comes from the mouth of the Lord in the Book of Revelations. You speak your life! You call forth the presence of God! You speak your emotions, for good or bad. This is a

MAY THE SEEDS OF DECEIT BE BLOWN AWAY LIKE CHAFF FROM THE WHEAT

great power of manifestation that is over looked by almost everyone.

What you ask is what you receive and the Universal law of Creation does not know when you are speaking for good or bad. All you say creates your life. So beware what you say. If you say I don't want something, the Universe does not recognize the negative words and hears this is what I want. So be careful how you phrase things. God doesn't care what you don't want, He hears what you want. For instance if you are ill, then ask for healing, but don't say God I don't want to be sick. Take out the word don't and see what you are asking for!

You have been given the keys to the Kingdom in this message. This is the five fingers of the hand of God that has been presented to you. Take this seriously!

Make this year your priority and make this your purpose. There is no halfway point because to be a faithful child of God, you must be obedient and stand steadfast. There is a way to do all things but you must put God first. If God is for you who can

ONE LIFE...ONE LOVE...ETERNAL

MAY THE SEEDS OF DECEIT BE BLOWN AWAY LIKE CHAFF FROM THE WHEAT

successfully stand against you. Be at peace in the arms of the Lord and know that you are loved!

ONE LIFE...ONE LOVE...ETERNAL

MAY THE SEEDS OF DECEIT BE BLOWN AWAY LIKE CHAFF FROM THE WHEAT

24 CREATION

The love of the Lord is with you today. Love is the greatest gift. No one can survive without love in their lives. People deprived of love as babies grow up to be murders, psychopaths, and sociopaths.

A person who lives cut off from the love of God will perish in the perils of the enemy. It is God's love that keeps you safe. It is up to each individual to seek the love and protection of the Lord.

Be at peace in the arms of the Lord. Know that you are loved and send your love, your praise and your gratitude up to God and bring down a rain of blessings into your life. Never doubt the love or God's intention for your life.

What you believe is created and happens. You forecast your future and you have created the life you are living today! Your life is dictated by you; the power of creation lies within the mind, the emotions and the tongue. Love and faith are the engine; creation lies within the tools.

If you want change, then you must change. If you want love, you must give love. You get what you give.

ONE LIFE...ONE LOVE...ETERNAL

<u>MAY THE SEEDS OF DECEIT BE BLOWN AWAY LIKE
CHAFF FROM THE WHEAT</u>

ONE LIFE...ONE LOVE...ETERNAL

25 GETTING TO THE WELL

To be loved by God is your greatest gift. If God did not love his children, these attempts to touch your heart would not have been written. The Lord is pleased with your progress. There are many who seek the Lord's guidance that wants to receive these lessons. If you are ignorant of God's vision for you, how can you fulfill what you were created to do? There are people who thirst for a drink, and do not know how to get to the well.

There is a path to the well. The way to find the path is through prayer and meditation. Prayer is essential for a spiritual relationship. How can you have a relationship with someone if you never speak to them?

Prayer is simply communicating your heart with your Father in Heaven. Speaking how you feel, stating what is bothering you, and what you want out of life will open the doorway for God to bless you. All that you need has been created by God and is waiting for you; all is ready for you! Think of it as everything is being held in a warehouse awaiting delivery instructions. Prayer places the order. That which you need is ready, all you have

MAY THE SEEDS OF DECEIT BE BLOWN AWAY LIKE CHAFF FROM THE WHEAT

to do is claim it, call it forth and do what is needed to receive.

Meditation is God's opportunity to talk to you. God does not want a one way conversation. Meditation is like tuning up your car. If you had an expensive luxury car, but you never cleaned it, put good fuel in it, or never did any maintenance; it wouldn't be a luxury car for very long! Regardless of the price of the treasure, if it isn't loved and maintained, it will lose its value to you. It is the same with the spiritual self; you need to clean your spiritual house, refuel your spirit, and allow the Holy Spirit to make adjustments and repairs to the body, the mind and the spirit

*<u>**Psalm 51:10   Create in me a clean house, O God; renew me in a right spirit within me**</u>*

26 PRAISE

Praise is your opportunity to tell your Father how you feel. If you love someone, you should tell them. God is attracted to your praise and worship. If you want to experience God's presence, the path is through praise.

Prayer sets you on the path, meditation opens up the consciousness to receive and praise takes you up the path to God's presence. That is the path the Bible teaches. You must come to the Father through this path. Christ Jesus taught that all must come to the Father through Him. Christ's sacrifice allowed us access to the Holy Spirit. When you conclude your prayer in the name of Christ Jesus you bring the blessings of the Son into your spiritual work.

> *St. John 10:1   Verily, verily I say unto you, he that enters not by the door into the sheepfold, but climbs up some other way, is the same is a thief and a robber.*
>
> *St. John 10:9-10   I (Jesus) am the door; if by me if any man enters in, he shall be saved, and*

MAY THE SEEDS OF DECEIT BE BLOWN AWAY LIKE CHAFF FROM THE WHEAT

> *shall go in and out, and find pasture... I have come that they might have life, and they might have it more abundantly.*

Beware of tarot cards, Ouija boards, runes, fortunetellers, etc., because they are that the Christ spoke of. These have open channels, which can lead to evil influences. Would you take guidance from a stranger just because they have a familiar spirit that communicates with them? You must be able to discern if what you are being told is of God and discernment comes only from the Holy Spirit.

Come to God through Christ and receive His blessings. Do not put your faith in other paths. The way is through Christ. The path is prayer, meditation and praise. God loves your love and your worship! You must be consistent to succeed. If you want relationship, if you want favor and blessings, then take this opportunity to grow in spirit. Take this message to heart and be at peace in the Lord.

ONE LIFE...ONE LOVE...ETERNAL

27 THE CALL TO BROTHERHOOD

The call to brotherhood is a call to unite the people of God, to come together for the lost and for the coming upheaval. There is a war coming and we must be prepared. There is work to be done, to pull this world out of darkness and back from the brink. People are living in hopelessness and need to be helped, who is willing to put away the denominations of religion that separate us and join together?

Can God rely on you? God needs mankind to work with Him to manifest His works on Earth. Man has dominion, so man must choose what works will be done. Man seems not to have a problem with doing the works of the enemy, even though those things are destructive to the self, the family and the world. The enemy offers temporary pleasures that will lead people to lie, cheat and steal to possess. What are you willing to do for God? Are you willing to unite to do his work? Can you be trusted with the works of God? In the works for Christ is the path to a whole new life.

If you love the supernatural, you're going to love being a Christian! Have you noticed how people are ready to believe the workings and the power

MAY THE SEEDS OF DECEIT BE BLOWN AWAY LIKE CHAFF FROM THE WHEAT

of evil? The world has work so hard to convince us that the supernatural is the domain of the enemy and that only the darkness holds the power. The enemy is afraid of the power that lies within Christ. We as a people have allowed Satan to lie and destroy long enough.

Through Christ lies true power, that is just waiting for you to open your heart and receive. Every time someone opens their eyes, looks to heaven and opens their heart the enemy quakes in his soul, because he is diminished! God is still in the miracle business and all he is waiting for is you. Christ is the most powerful man who ever walked the world, He walked in service to others, to bring the word and the truth to the world! Jesus would work miracles and told people to tell no one but to go to the Temple and give thanks to our Father for the work that was done for Him, in His name and for His glory.

God speaks to us and God shows us the way. He performs miracles for us. He can heal us and he can transform us. Money can be manifested in times of need and the words you need to communicate will come to you. God is calling us to establish a new age of God which will be the falling away of the divisions of religion, to allow

ONE LIFE...ONE LOVE...ETERNAL

MAY THE SEEDS OF DECEIT BE BLOWN AWAY LIKE CHAFF FROM THE WHEAT

the teachings of God to take priority over the designs and ideas of man.

This is an effort to reach out to those people who question the concepts of dogma and just want to know and understand God. The people of been led astray by the very ones who call themselves leaders and teachers. Please give these messages a chance and see if they touch your heart, your mind and your spirit. This is the accumulation of one person's life in seeking the truth through prayer and meditation and the will of God. What will it hurt to receive these words of encouragement?

ONE LIFE...ONE LOVE...ETERNAL

MAY THE SEEDS OF DECEIT BE BLOWN AWAY LIKE CHAFF FROM THE WHEAT

28 SLEEPWALKERS

The Lord is with you today. The people are so lost! They are like the zombies that they love so much. They are wandering aimlessly, without being aware, all the while looking for something, afraid to think and afraid to worship. All they want is to be entertained, they expect God to entertain them and that is not how it works. They must entertain God to receive his presence.

Satan is the great entertainer, singing sweet songs of lies to keep the masses distracted.

There is more to what we are attracted to the just something to humor us. Zombies are mindless walking dead that feast on the flesh of innocent people. Vampires are walking dead that thrive on the blood of people. Each has no conscience and no moral rules. They are not answerable to anyone or anything; the world is theirs for the taking.

Isn't that the same lies that the deceiver wants us to believe? If you want to have a life of miracles and joy you have to choose what you want to do with your spare time. Miracles await all who seek! Peace is found in the practice of communing with the presence of the Holy Spirit. Call it whatever

ONE LIFE...ONE LOVE...ETERNAL

MAY THE SEEDS OF DECEIT BE BLOWN AWAY LIKE CHAFF FROM THE WHEAT

you want, but know that all receive through the Holy Spirit. It is the channel of love between the realms.

ONE LIFE...ONE LOVE...ETERNAL

MAY THE SEEDS OF DECEIT BE BLOWN AWAY LIKE CHAFF FROM THE WHEAT

29 MIRACLES

Miracles await all who seek. Peace is found in the practice of communing with the Holy Spirit. You can call God's presence whatever you want, but know that all that receive do so through the Holy Spirit. It is the channel of love between these realms.

The love is the greatest miracle. To be loved is the gift God gives to the multitude. To be a child of the highest God is a continuing miracle. There is a guide for each individual; they dedicate their existence to the progress of their beloved charges. The Father of us all wants us to evolve and shake off the generational curses that have been inherited through the ages.

Contamination of the DNA has increased with each generation. Like a virus it sits within ready to take over. Through the influence of the Holy Spirit these contaminations can be cleaned out and repaired.

The Holy Spirit realigns the spiritual body with the human body and brings healing and elimination of the negative influences. This is a process that makes the new man in Christ. Every step you take to God is a healing and a bonding.

ONE LIFE...ONE LOVE...ETERNAL

MAY THE SEEDS OF DECEIT BE BLOWN AWAY LIKE CHAFF FROM THE WHEAT

JEREMIAH 33:3 CALL UNTO ME, AND I WILL ANSWER YOU, AND SHOW YOU GREAT AND MIGHTY THINGS, WHICH YOU KNOW NOT.

30 ALIGNMENT

Hebrews 11:6 but without faith it is impossible to please Him: for he that comes to God must believe that He is, and that he is the rewarder of them that diligently seek Him.

ONE LIFE...ONE LOVE...ETERNAL

MAY THE SEEDS OF DECEIT BE BLOWN AWAY LIKE CHAFF FROM THE WHEAT

The love of God is with you today. When you try to find alignment, there are obstacles to overcome. You will need to watch what you watch; these influences are the emotions, the way your mind reacts to things and the hormone levels produced in the body. What you eat, drink and do all influence these hormones and how the mind works. Stimulants such as drugs are destructive to the process of alignment and to the body. Alcohol is a drug as well but it can calm unless it is abused. The effects of alcohol abuse on the body are destructive. It harms all parts of the body and it especially affects the brain causing a chemical imbalance which causes depression.

Tobacco is a stimulant and harms the whole body. Many people are trying to stop this addiction. Through strength and faith; both in the self and in God will help you overcome this obstacle. Whatever desire exists for the addiction through prayer you can receive healing.

Seek a balance in all things. Modify your food, decrease the sugar and feed the body the nutrients you need. Your guides are there to help. The stronger the faith, the greater the connection, the easier it will be to stop any destructive behavior.

ONE LIFE...ONE LOVE...ETERNAL

MAY THE SEEDS OF DECEIT BE BLOWN AWAY LIKE CHAFF FROM THE WHEAT

You are loved beyond comprehension. Peace can be yours. Seek harmony in your life. All things are possible through God. You must believe, maintain your communion with God throughout the cleansing and the adjustment of the habit. With compassion for all you see and through love all things can be changed for the betterment of the world. Today is your gift. Your life is a gift so use it; don't sleep throughout your day. Be aware of your body, what you are doing and what you are thinking. Stop the negative parade of thoughts that haunt the mind. Recognize them and replace them with positive thoughts. Focus on God and eliminate those things that hurt you.

31 ALIGNMENT: THE 1ST STEP

The love of God is with you. Today is a gift. The love of God is your greatest gift. There are many gifts you take for granted. What would you do if God decided you did not need his gifts because you take them and show no gratitude?

There are many steps you must take for unity. The most important is commitment. You must commit yourself to growing your faith. You must devote time to focus on your spiritual growth. Start each day with a prayer. Show God you are grateful for

MAY THE SEEDS OF DECEIT BE BLOWN AWAY LIKE CHAFF FROM THE WHEAT

another day. Ask God to be with you and to guide you and to show him your will. Take a few moments before your day takes over to clear your mind and meditate on the Fathers will. Plan your day and see how it will go smoothly. Plan on a day of peace and joy and this will set your mind on the proper path. Know what you need to do and have a process that will give you flow.

If you will begin each day with a prayer and express your gratitude; then seek knowledge, wisdom and guidance in your sleep time, you will see a tremendous change in your daily life. No caffeine after six in the evening. Center yourself in peace at the end of the day. If you have concerns give them to the Lord, ask for resolution and release them. You will be supplied with a solution at the proper time.

The spiritual self has access to God consciousness. While you are sleeping or going about your day the spirit self will work out the solution and it will come to you as an inspiration. All that you need is already created in the spiritual realm; it is up to you to claim what is provided for you. Only what you need is provided; only what is good for you. Unanswered prayers are one of our greatest gifts.

ONE LIFE...ONE LOVE...ETERNAL

MAY THE SEEDS OF DECEIT BE BLOWN AWAY LIKE CHAFF FROM THE WHEAT

See who you want to be in God, see the new man in God, and bring him into focus. Practice this in your life. See what God has in store for you! Thank God for all you are. Praise will bring you closer to God. Gratitude and love call forth his favor and his presence.

Seek to be a person of God. May the peace of the Lord be yours today!

ONE LIFE...ONE LOVE...ETERNAL

32 MEDITATION

To you the love is given. Those who seek the Lord will hear the call for truth. Much of the world is under the assumption that the days are gone when God spoke to his children. There needs to come a time when God can be heard by all who follow.

There needs to be a focus on centering the mind, body and spirit on God. This allows God to heal and change the heart. This also allows the mind to accept new principles and recognize them as truth.

Meditation on the Lord simply means clearing out all distractions for a short time and focusing on God. Clearing the mind allows God to touch your inner being. Focus on God, your love for him and your desire to feel his touch within.

Heaven is filled with pure white light; there is no darkness or shadow. Focus on that heavenly light and have it fill your mind. Bring the light into the body at the top of the head and have it flow through every cell. Feel the light permeating every cell every atom, and feel the healing and the

MAY THE SEEDS OF DECEIT BE BLOWN AWAY LIKE CHAFF FROM THE WHEAT

peace that will permeate the body, the mind and the spirit. The light can heal the heart of passed wounds, heal the body of disease and repair damage. The light can build up your spirit and bring balance to the mind-body connection. This is something that will require practice and dedication. When you precede meditation with devotional prayer you can find a harmony and peace that can be the center of your day.

Daily morning meditation will allow you to start your day in peace and joy. You are beginning your day in faith and devotion; preparing the soul for your day. Once you finish, give thanks and take a minute to visualize your day, to get what you want to accomplish set in motion. This sets the universe into alignment with what you expect. You need to have goals and desires to succeed in life. Your desire sets the emotion for what you want, the things you want to accomplish. Your goals focus the mind on where you are going.

Contemplate what you want. Compose a list of nine things you want to happen. Things you want to receive, things you want to accomplish and things you want to resolve. Read this list daily as a petition to God and just wait until you see the results. As each petition comes into being deleted

ONE LIFE...ONE LOVE...ETERNAL

MAY THE SEEDS OF DECEIT BE BLOWN AWAY LIKE CHAFF FROM THE WHEAT

from the list and add a new petition to the bottom of the list.

Let this become a daily ritual preferably morning and night and you will be amazed at the results. The universe was set in motion to supply all that we need and it's up to you to call what you need into being. I pray that this will touch your heart and you will start a routine that will change your life and call forth miracles. Know that you are loved and may the peace of Christ be with you today.

ONE LIFE...ONE LOVE...ETERNAL

<u>May the Seeds of Deceit be Blown Away Like Chaff from the Wheat</u>

33 Holy Spirit

The Lord is with you today. The Holy Spirit is the voice of God to His children. The Holy Spirit is the deliverer of miracles to the initiated. The Holy Spirit is the voice of the deliverer of the message. To be loved is the greatest gift. The Holy Spirit comes to those who live for God and are willing to receive the gifts of the spirit.

To be a warrior for the world you must put yourself in God's hands. Only God knows the time and the place for action. You must be a full-time warrior in faith for the Father; know He is with you.

Holy, holy, holy is the Father of us all, the Lord God on high who is the creator of the Universe. Your Fathers devotion never wavers; He never turns away from you. You must be a receiver of the word. You must be faithful. Just as Jesus told the disciples to be faithful and to know that He was with them, you must understand, you must know, He is with you.

Do not turn away your face from the light. God will not honor those that do not honor him. God will not guide you into darkness. If you are tested, it will not be more than you can bear. The light

MAY THE SEEDS OF DECEIT BE BLOWN AWAY LIKE CHAFF FROM THE WHEAT

will always be with you. The Holy Spirit is your doorway to communion with God.

God needs you to open your heart in faith and acceptance of the gift of the Lord's Holy Spirit. You must seek the face of God and only through your love and devotion can you receive the holy touch of God. To progress spiritually, you must lay the foundation of faith, prayer and praise so that you may build your house of faith. Christ Jesus is the shelter that surrounds you. The Holy Spirit is the one that fills that house with God's love. Seek the Father through love and you will receive the love in return, beyond your understanding. To seek the Holy Spirit is your quest! Believe in the love of God, it is your greatest gift. It is through love and only through love, that you receive the touch of God through the Holy Spirit.

Meditate only on God, no mantras except the Father of us all. Focus on God, God's love and God's guidance. If you accept the quest, you will reap the reward. Be at peace in the Lord.

You must know and understand that all who have life have a spirit. The spirit is the life force to the body. When the spirit departs, the body is left lifeless. Just as you must feed the body with food and water, then you must feed the spirit.

ONE LIFE...ONE LOVE...ETERNAL

MAY THE SEEDS OF DECEIT BE BLOWN AWAY LIKE CHAFF FROM THE WHEAT

When you decide to dedicate your life to Christ, you are agreeing to accept the will of God in your life. This starts a process of change within the spirit and the consciousness. This is the beginning of a covenant you have made with the creator. You must keep this renewal in the forefront of your life, if you are to make the changes required to become a new person in Christ and to be able to receive the gifts of the Holy Spirit.

Your covenant is precious and delicate. It must be new nurtured like a small child, so it may grow into adulthood and only through communion with the Holy Spirit will you be able to succeed. This is an agreement based in love because it's your love of God which has moved you to dedicate your life to Christ. The love of the Father for his child offers you this precious gift. The gift comes with joy, relationship and communion with God, through the spiritual bond you have made. This is the path to God and the more you focus on God, the more you show your love and dedication, the stronger the connection will become. It is vital you nourish this holy communion of God, if you are to stay on the narrow path, which leads to a life of joy and abundance.

ONE LIFE...ONE LOVE...ETERNAL

MAY THE SEEDS OF DECEIT BE BLOWN AWAY LIKE CHAFF FROM THE WHEAT

You are in a Valley and you want to climb the mountain that stands before you. The mountain is rocky and dangerous, but there is one safe path that leads to the top. If you look closely, you will see a narrow path that leads upward. All you need for this journey is a light to guide you.

> *St. John 8:12   I am the light of the world: he that follows me shall not walk in darkness, but shall have the light of life.*

Your covenant with God is your light and it will show you the way, because the way is easy if you stay on the narrow path as you climb. To become distracted and stray from the path is dangerous. Your guidance and protection is on the path. If you wander away from the path, don't be discouraged and give up. God's not going to give up on you because his grace and forgiveness are always there for you. The Lord knows your weaknesses and will patiently wait for you to come back to your purpose.

Much is said about obedience and this seems to rub people the wrong way, because the image of a dog going through obedience training comes to mind, but that is not what we are referring to. You

MAY THE SEEDS OF DECEIT BE BLOWN AWAY LIKE CHAFF FROM THE WHEAT

can train an animal to act in a certain way, when you are with them, but when they are alone they revert to their own instincts. You can't teach an animal the difference between right and wrong, only man has been blessed with an inner conscience that allows us to make choices. That small inner voice that speaks guidance and truth is the Holy Spirit gently guiding you on the path. You will come to know the gentle touch of the Spirit of God as you begin to respond to the urgings and directions.

Obedience is simply listening to the Spirit of God within and making the right choices when challenges come before you. The enemy of man knows all our weaknesses and what affects us. If we submit to temptations, then we will become bombarded with guilt and regret. When become flooded with feelings of unworthiness, we begin to dwell on our shortcomings. Don't allow yourself to be drawn into this drama, playing it over and over in your mind.

Forgiveness is the answer; you are forgiven the second you admit to the Lord that you made a mistake, you are forgiven! Repentance is nothing more than admitting we messed up and learning the lesson. The moment you take it to God, you

MAY THE SEEDS OF DECEIT BE BLOWN AWAY LIKE CHAFF FROM THE WHEAT

are forgiven, but the catch is you have to forgive yourself and let yourself off the hook. Make it right as best you can, if you hurt someone go to them and ask their forgiveness. If you only hurt yourself, then make it right within and move on. Each day is a new beginning, if you allow it to be. This is how God shows His love, through Grace. You are a cherished and loved child of God. Be at peace.

34 ATTUNEMENT TO THE HOLY SPIRIT

The Lord is with you today. Be at peace in the Lord God's love. There are many levels of attunement with the Holy Spirit. Once you open the portal of the God force, you begin a new journey and the Holy Spirit will guide you and lead you to new revelations and new abilities. The gifts of the Holy Spirit will come to you as you evolve in faith and believing. There are gifts that allow you to navigate the human realm and other gifts that allow you to evolve spiritually.

The human realm requires you to be steadfast and single-minded. You must train yourself to navigate the world and not fall into the distraction of the world. The evolution of the spirit comes from communion with the Holy Spirit, which builds your inner strength. To be able to reach out and receive the touch of God at any time is the goal. The gifts of the spirit of God are the way you become a warrior and a watcher for God. Anytime challenges come before you, they are temptations; just as Christ Jesus was tempted in the desert. How you handle these challenges are direct reflections on your spiritual strength. Do

MAY THE SEEDS OF DECEIT BE BLOWN AWAY LIKE CHAFF FROM THE WHEAT

not be pulled into the cesspool of the world! We are called to be in the world but not to be of the world and its ways.

The members of mankind that have refused the Lord have pulled the devices of the enemy into the Paradise that is the earth. The lost souls have attached themselves to the ego and the desires of Lucifer and have rained hell down upon earth.

Through God and God alone can we walk through the muck and stay clean. We'll walk in the light while the lost wallow in the dark. The gifts are your armor against their influence. When you stand in the light, all the influences of the dark will scurry away, back into the shadows.

Take notice how some people cannot stand to be near people of faith. The enemy owns their heart and mind and will pull them away. They will be angry and they will attempt to curse you. With each rejection of the light they fall farther and farther into darkness. Until they cry out in the darkness for the Lord they will be lost. Each time they are exposed to the light they are given a new chance.

Love and compassion for the lost is your greatest weapon against the dark. These are part of the

ONE LIFE...ONE LOVE...ETERNAL

MAY THE SEEDS OF DECEIT BE BLOWN AWAY LIKE CHAFF FROM THE WHEAT

shield of the warrior. Every time you offer understanding, compassion and pray for the lost you help to bring them to the light. Prayer is your weapon against the enemy of mankind. The enemy of mankind has forces that are united against God. God's children must all learn to be united!

- Stop being self-righteous; this is a weapon that the enemy uses to destroy you.
- Stop judging other Christians; the enemy uses this to destroy our brotherhood.
- Stop questioning your faith; this diminishes your progress.

Follow the teachings of Christ Jesus and learn to discern the truth. The war is coming! You must have your armor ready. You must build a steadfast heart and mind. The war is for our life, the life of your family and for your right to walk in the light. The enemy wants to strip the earth from God and make his hell on earth our existence.

The joy comes in building your relationship and the peace of the Lord comes with love, faith and trust. There is a hunger that can only be fed by the Holy Spirit. True love is only felt when you are touched by God's benevolent spirit. Earthly love is

ONE LIFE...ONE LOVE...ETERNAL

MAY THE SEEDS OF DECEIT BE BLOWN AWAY LIKE CHAFF FROM THE WHEAT

only a mirror reflection of the love of the Father. Somewhat like looking at your image in a pool of water, which is just a mirror image of the real thing.

In God's realm there is no darkness; there is no fear because there is only love. The love of God is beyond human comprehension. Know that you are loved and God is waiting for you to show him you want his love, guidance and protection. Love is eternal, it does not die, and it goes with us when we graduate from this life to the next. Our consciousness is preserved throughout eternity!

We are created with our purpose and that is all we need to fulfill our destiny that God is laid out for us. This is a matter of agreement before we are even born. We are intact spiritually throughout eternity and when we return to the realm of God, we must give explanation for our lives and evaluate our works. The works we perform here go with us. Don't waste your life chasing temporary things; we are here for just a little while, so make the most of your life and know this, love is the key to a successful life, not what your bank balance is at your passing. Remember all that you do know that you are

ONE LIFE...ONE LOVE...ETERNAL

loved and you are never alone. May the peace of the Lord influence your life!

35 THE Devine way

The Lord is with you today. To be loved is the greatest gift. New levels of understanding are coming to the seekers. Many of the lost are there because they were never taught to love God. More and more are looking for a better way to live. These people need joy and guidance. They need to know they are loved to help the world make sense.

If you have no purpose, then you are just wandering aimlessly in the world. If you don't know where you are going or how to get there then you are lost. If you do not live in love and peace then you are lost. Render your heart and open it to the Holy Spirit, which is provided to all who seek.

Once you find your unity with the spirit you will find a peace and harmony within because you are no longer alone. You will know there is more to life than the here and now. You will see the spirit is eternal, always to be part of God's realm. You are not an accident; not an accidental collection of

MAY THE SEEDS OF DECEIT BE BLOWN AWAY LIKE CHAFF FROM THE WHEAT

atoms that happened to find consciousness. God is the scientist that created it all and made the laws of nature and man.

Man is made above all else; given free will, self-awareness that has made you the dominant species. That makes the earth your responsibility. You are responsible and answerable for what you do. The lesson is here if you choose to receive. If you allow others to lead you into darkness, you cannot give away the responsibility. Choose carefully who you follow.

Many people use the state of the world as proof that God doesn't exist. They cry out, if there is a God, why does He allow the abominations of the world to continue? Why does He allow so many different religions? Here is the reason:

When God created Adam he gave dominion (rule) over the Earth. When God mandates a law, even He can't break it. Only through the flesh of man can God work. Free will is a double edged sword that can do evil as well as good. If you decide to allow Satan to work through you, instead of God, that is your choice. Not until you pass from the flesh to the realm of the spirit, will you be answerable for your acts. Regardless of whose name you act in, it is your choice! Make sure you

MAY THE SEEDS OF DECEIT BE BLOWN AWAY LIKE CHAFF FROM THE WHEAT

follow the mandates of Christ before you act. False leaders and prophets will abound and you will have to discern the truth.

If you choose to follow a dogma that calls on you to harm others it is a false dogma. End the hatred between the tribes of man. To hate is to grieve the Father. Hatred is the enemy of man. The enemy uses the spirit of self-righteousness to manipulate the ego and the emotions. The greatest lies have a message of truth that has been woven with deceit. This feeds the emotions and fuels retribution. No one is perfectly right in their religion. The seed of love is there, but then the intolerance is woven in and they separate themselves into sects, using their faith to judge others and placing themselves above all others. Christ taught love and tolerance. If the true doctrine of the Father was taught and followed there would be an explosion of faith all around the planet!

Study what Christ said. Look at what Christ did in three years. Follow the teaching set forth by the Father. What could you do in 20 years if you would accept the messianic spirit into your life and followed through to the end? Blessings are there for the follower of the spirit. Miracles are

ONE LIFE...ONE LOVE...ETERNAL

MAY THE SEEDS OF DECEIT BE BLOWN AWAY LIKE CHAFF FROM THE WHEAT

waiting for you in God's realm for you to reach up and claim for your own. Be at peace today and know that the Lord is with you.

36 THE Coming Tribulation

When you set yourself aside, and you allow God to speak is a great thing and to submit to God's will instead of your own this too is a great thing. We have asked much of this woman and she keeps saying, yes Lord I will do my best. Let the world hear the voice of the Father of the universe! There is a lack of dedication to God. The whole world hears its own voice, not the voice of the Father. They kill in their own name not mine. They sit in judgment in my place, in self-righteousness not for me but to make them superior. My children you must stop!!! I will not honor you, if you do not honor me. I will not put you first, if I am not first. My protection falls on those who are in my family. You see not all of mankind is in my family. All are welcome, but to be as my own you will have to be accepted.

Acceptance is based on love. If you cannot love me above all else; if you cannot love another as yourself, you will not be accepted!

There is a hunger in man that he has interpreted as ambition, and he tries to fill that hunger with success. Are you never satisfied? Are you never grateful? When will you have enough that you can

MAY THE SEEDS OF DECEIT BE BLOWN AWAY LIKE CHAFF FROM THE WHEAT

rest? There is a way to do all things and keep God at your center.

There is a way through prayer, meditation and submission to God's will, to live a life of peace and contentment. There is a way to live a life of love. There is a way to succeed in life without worshiping money, cars, houses and prestige. Money is not evil, greed is evil

The hate that is growing in the Middle East is going to overflow onto the world. They will cause the wrath of the Enemy to rain down on all of mankind. The government will offer a solution. First they will try to disarm everyone, in the name of a peaceful solution. They will begin by requesting the chip in everyone so they can locate the subversive element when they act up, but soon it will be required. All that they will offer will be presented as a peaceful solution to the terrorism. The people will welcome this with open arms because they have been unwilling to see the truth and understand the prophecy that God has laid before you and the Book of Revelations so that you may see what is coming.

This is all mapped out by those who operate in the enemy's army. They honestly believe they can offer a solution and peace which will be under one

MAY THE SEEDS OF DECEIT BE BLOWN AWAY LIKE CHAFF FROM THE WHEAT

authority, without God (you see they're going to blame all of the upheaval and all the turmoil on God) to live in peace. The peace they are offering is for all to be like robots, obeying the orders of their masters, who will sit on the throne above everyone and declare himself God on earth.

If you choose to worship God, you will be cast from society. You will live a life of persecution, ridicule and hate. They will attack your faith, calling it superstition and weakness. Worship will be conducted underground, hidden for protection. Many today who are professing to be of faith, will fall when the test is given. They believe the rapture will be there salvation and they will not be tested. When this does not come true their faith will fall.

The Lord knows the heart, the strength and the will of each individual. The strength of your faith must be built up now. You must see the danger, the time of tribulation is upon every person and there can be no turning back.

The hearts of man have been turned to stone and the mind rages and cries out for blood. Defiance is the path to ruin. Prayer, meditation and faith are needed to survive the tide of blood that is coming.

ONE LIFE...ONE LOVE...ETERNAL

MAY THE SEEDS OF DECEIT BE BLOWN AWAY LIKE CHAFF FROM THE WHEAT

Please remember the Lord is with you today and wants you to be blessed and all that you do, but you must remember to keep God first and foremost in your life if you are to survive the next decade. I love you all.

ONE LIFE....ONE LOVE....ETERNAL

MAY THE SEEDS OF DECEIT BE BLOWN AWAY LIKE CHAFF FROM THE WHEAT

37 THE OPEN VESSEL

This is the day the Lord God, Father of us all made. To love God is an easy thing all that is required is a heart that is seeking an open to God's touch. Are you an open vessel, or are you so full of your own world that there is no place for God?

A relationship is based on knowing one another, trust and love. God already knows you, trust you, because he knows who you really are and he loves you as only a father can. You are presently carrying around the past and you are busy worrying about the future. So tell me this, where is there room for today? Where are you residing; in the past, present or the future?

The past is gone, it cannot be changed and the future is beyond your control. Who you are right now, is who you are. If you want to change your future you must act today. You see God for gave you before you ever even asked. You see you know your weaknesses and he knows your expectations. Did you know you get what you expect? Expect lack and lack will be yours. Expect change and you will receive change. But you will have to take the first step in faith for it to happen and with each step will lead to another.

ONE LIFE...ONE LOVE...ETERNAL

MAY THE SEEDS OF DECEIT BE BLOWN AWAY LIKE CHAFF FROM THE WHEAT

Each step is a success! Every day you believe, more and more in yourself and as long as you are going along following God's purpose for you because that is where you must be. Just as Judy's path is to write, yours lies before you. The path is easy but it is when you stray from the narrow path that difficulties will arise.

This is being written to help you find your purpose and to teach you where your path lies. The way is narrow to your benefit. The banquet that you are to receive is beyond imagining.

The tree of life bears 12 fruits. The fruits nourish and replenish your spiritual self. If you will sit at God's table, you will be fed the fruits of life and be given living waters to drink. In our lifetime there are Millennia's passing on earth. We watch you from the time you decide to be born until you return to us. If you live to be 100 years old you are still an infant to God. Would you condemn your child before it knows the difference between what is right and what is wrong?

That is why you are expected to mess up, because only then can you learn. 100 lessons can be learned by failure. One lesson is taught by success and that is to repeat what you have done.

ONE LIFE...ONE LOVE...ETERNAL

MAY THE SEEDS OF DECEIT BE BLOWN AWAY LIKE CHAFF FROM THE WHEAT

If a person is given all they need, why would they strive for more? If you were born perfect, with complete understanding of God, then why would you need to come here? You would be glorified and desire to stay in perfection. If you are alive on planet Earth you are a student. You must watch every moment, guard your heart from the evil of the world and learn.

Until you can say no to the Devil, you are not qualified to say yes I am ready to come home. Choices abound from awakening to sleep. What you choose is up to you. You can choose to sleep on! What to eat? Where you go? All are choices that set your day. It might seem simple, but every choice has an outcome. Feed your body junk and feel moody all day and within hour or two you are hungry again.

Your body is a miracle of chemistry and physics. It must be treated well and fed well. Abuse is easy; the narrow diet leads to health. Limit sugar, no processed foods, and natural foods only. Better life through chemistry is a lie.

Cancer is raging because of better chemistry such as fluoride in your drinking water, dyes and preservatives. Diabetes is next, the imbalance of hormones and sugar. Obesity comes from bad

ONE LIFE...ONE LOVE...ETERNAL

MAY THE SEEDS OF DECEIT BE BLOWN AWAY LIKE CHAFF FROM THE WHEAT

decisions, bad thoughts and bad foods. Diabetes is a symptom of greed, a hunger for more. The narrow diet is fruits and nuts and grains all has God made them how long would it take to clean up your diet? Red meat causes anger and aggressive behavior. Its best left alone but all natural is better but only once a week. The items of the flesh are being poisoned by the food they are fed, the living conditions and hormones they are given. We understand this is not easy to do. Contamination is in the air, the soil and the water. Autism is diet related. Most of the diseases today are from food. All you can do is rely on the best you can buy. Be at peace. All is not lost. You can do this, one small step at a time.

To all who have eyes, see the truth!! To all who have ears, hear the truth!! Let the lies of man be blown away as chaff is blown from the wheat! Know that you are loved today beyond all understanding that is why the Lord is reaching out to you in this way. Be at peace.

ONE LIFE...ONE LOVE...ETERNAL

38 GOD'S MANDATE TO HIS CHILDREN

The Lord is with you today. There is a great work to be done. This will require you to remember your purpose. You will have to dedicate yourself to follow God's mandate.

> **The mandate of God:** To love the Lord thy God above all others, even beyond the love of the self. You are to honor God in all that you do and to place your life in the hands of your creator.

There is a disease that is infected the world. It is the disease of self-worship. Every sentence has the word me in it! If your world consists of the words I, me, and mine, then you are infected. Take a minute, to think about your attitude. If you are not loved enough, then you do not love enough. If you are not receiving, then you are not giving.

All that you worship and strive to hold onto will fly away from you! Anything you wish to have you must honor it, respect it, but do not covet. That is why God commands you not to covet. Every

MAY THE SEEDS OF DECEIT BE BLOWN AWAY LIKE CHAFF FROM THE WHEAT

commandment is not there to limit you but to protect you.

If you watch what is happening in the world, you will see things are getting worse. Things that were created in covenant with God have been abandoned their promise. If you make a covenant with God, you are protected if you break covenant with God; you leave the protection and guidance of the Father of us all. Christ died and was reborn into eternity for you. Christ paid the price to give you grace.

You have taken grace to be a ticket to do whatever you want because you are under grace. This is blasphemy! You cannot be perfect, but you can do your best to grow and to learn. Salvation and grace are precious and you throw them into the pig sty until you need God's mercy and help. You are to treasure your salvation and grace and be grateful. Show your heart to God.

The story of the prodigal son was of a man who coveted his inheritance and the world. He wanted to live! He walked away from his Father and gave no more thought to his father until...

The riches he coveted flew from him, the people he chose over his Father, took his money, stole for

MAY THE SEEDS OF DECEIT BE BLOWN AWAY LIKE CHAFF FROM THE WHEAT

him and when it was all gone they mocked and spat upon him.

Not until he was working to feed the swine and he was being forced to eat with the pigs that he finally realized that in his father's house even the lowest of the servants had shelter, food and love. This is when he decided to return to the protection of his **Father's House**. He was welcomed with open arms and never again did he stray from his Father.

Don't wait until you have sacrificed everything to the world. If you value your life, the life of your family and your future please take heed to this word from God

ONE LIFE...ONE LOVE...ETERNAL

MAY THE SEEDS OF DECEIT BE BLOWN AWAY LIKE CHAFF FROM THE WHEAT

39 A SIGN OF GOD'S FRUSTRATION WITH MAN

The Lord is with you today. Be at peace in the love of the Father of us all. The world is losing its way and following into darkness. This is an effort of the Father to use the love of one woman to reach out and touch those who are willing to receive the message of the Lord.

Christ Jesus came to change the minds of man and to help the people to see the way of the light of God. Man ignored the message and the way and built a religion. God's religion is love. God's message is love. Love one another, no matter what!

Love does not mean you agree; just know that all you can do is love them. Study the words of Christ Jesus. All that Christ Jesus did you can do. All the love of God is yours. Just as the universe is limitless, so is God's love. God makes the rules that govern the universe and mankind. God gave you dominion and you have thrown that gift away. God gave you the power of Christ Jesus through his sacrifice and you threw that gift away! When will you decide to take your rightful position in the Lord God's Kingdom?

ONE LIFE...ONE LOVE...ETERNAL

<u>MAY THE SEEDS OF DECEIT BE BLOWN AWAY LIKE
CHAFF FROM THE WHEAT</u>

ONE LIFE...ONE LOVE...ETERNAL

MAY THE SEEDS OF DECEIT BE BLOWN AWAY LIKE CHAFF FROM THE WHEAT

40 GOALS AND CHOICES

The Lord is here for you today. Keep your eyes focused on the goals you have made. Make God your partner in your quest. The one you can always rely on to help you, to guide you and love you is the Lord.

You must set goals to make progress. It's not enough to dream, to visualize or affirm if you do not set goals and figure out the steps to achieve those goals, you cannot succeed.

If you say I want to be a leader of man but you don't lead how will you succeed? If you say I want to start a new business, but all you do is watch TV and wait for God, how will you start this work? You need to know:

- what kind of work you want to do
- what you will need to do this work
- who you will work with
- what you will provide

Set goals that you can achieve. Small steps can lead you on a long journey. Just as this is true in business the same is true with God. First you set your heart on becoming closer with God. Then you start by keeping God on your mind, residing in

ONE LIFE...ONE LOVE...ETERNAL

MAY THE SEEDS OF DECEIT BE BLOWN AWAY LIKE CHAFF FROM THE WHEAT

the Lord's presence and focusing on your goal to receive the presence of the Holy Spirit.

Be aware of the small things that change within you and around you.

First you receive the possibility of God in your life. Then you start to see and acknowledge the Lord around you.

The next step is to accept the Lord into your life and accept his love and his grace. After that you must realize the old life and see your mistakes. You must ask the Lord to take these mistakes, guilt, scars because you must all and give them to God. God has already forgiven you, but to receive that forgiveness you must realize who you were and you must forgive yourself.

The next step is to forgive all who have hurt you. Forgiveness is the key to healing!

Once you have done these steps you can become a new person in Christ Jesus and begin your real-life. Your new man will have a new Holy name in the records of God. Be aware that with your new life come challenges. The old person will try to come back. Old patterns and thoughts will try to return. You will have to keep your eyes on God.

ONE LIFE...ONE LOVE...ETERNAL

MAY THE SEEDS OF DECEIT BE BLOWN AWAY LIKE CHAFF FROM THE WHEAT

The Lord will deliver you from that old person, but change takes time.

Just as being a drug addict can be cured in an instant by God or an alcoholic can be cured of his thirst for the drink, you too can be healed of whatever of affects you. The real challenge comes and living your life after the cure. Stopping old patterns and learning to live the life that you have accepted takes time and patience. Know that if you stumble or if you fall all you have to do is get up and start over again. Christ healed the leper's but only two stopped, turned around and returned to give him thanks to give him the glory. Only two out of 10 will keep this walk in the Lord, because they will forget why they have decided to take this path and they will allow the old man to surface.

Many people come to Christ for help when they are in a crisis. They call out to God for help, for their lives and for their families. Once everything is healed and life goes back to normal, then they forget their tears and they forget their deliverance. Very few take the time to give God the glory for the miracles that God performs in their lives.

ONE LIFE...ONE LOVE...ETERNAL

MAY THE SEEDS OF DECEIT BE BLOWN AWAY LIKE CHAFF FROM THE WHEAT

Be faithful to God. Be a blessing to those around you. Keep your heart on God's love and God's plan for you. Rise above the chaff and be in the ranks of those that the Lord blesses with his everlasting love and presence. God's love is the greatest gift to his children. You must accept your inheritance and claim your position as a child of the highest God, the holiest of holies, the Father of us all! Accept the Holy Spirit into your life. Except the spirit of Christ to influence your life and change the way you see your life. The Christ spirit is the messianic force of the universe. It is the mantle of love. The robe of righteousness is the garment that God gives to his children. It is the love of God for mankind. Whoever you are, whatever you think you are... God knows you. You are a part of the God force and you must accept the fact that you are part of that spirit. To live without acceptance of the spirit, you will not be able to be one of the chosen to fulfill the purpose you were born to.

We will be waiting for you to make your choice. Your Angels await your call. The spirit of God must be called upon, focused upon and commune with to evolve into the intended person you are destined to be.

ONE LIFE...ONE LOVE...ETERNAL

MAY THE SEEDS OF DECEIT BE BLOWN AWAY LIKE CHAFF FROM THE WHEAT

God is calling, will you answer? Be at peace in the Lord.

You are loved just as you are.

ONE LIFE...ONE LOVE...ETERNAL

41 LIVING IN THE NOW

The Lord is with you today. New levels of alignment can be attained through consistent prayer and meditation. It is not unusual that God speaks to certain people. It is possible for everyone to attain the gift of receiving. You must show the Lord your desire and dedication. Your love for the Father draws the precious Holy Spirit nearer. Many people hear God through intuition, inspiration, dreams and visions.

Pray out loud. When you pray out loud the vibrational field around you adjusts to the love you put into your prayer. It is vital that you allow the emotion that you feel in your heart to be heard. The mind believes as truth, what the mouth says. The tongue is your tool to use. Beware of what you say, you can do as much harm to yourself and others as you can do good.

Become a transmitter of love and peace to those around you. Choose the emotions that you send out. Choose the thoughts you allow in your mind. You can control your emotions if you choose to! You control your life. Life does not control you, just because things are going badly, just stop and take a few deep breaths, find your control and tell

MAY THE SEEDS OF DECEIT BE BLOWN AWAY LIKE CHAFF FROM THE WHEAT

yourself that you can change the situation and bring your joy back. Ask God for help and inspiration. Many times just being aware of what's happening around you will bring you back into the flow. Don't allow circumstances to control you. Control your circumstances!

If someone is condemning you falsely, do not fight them. What they think will not kill you. The truth will win out in the end. You are not what others think of you. You decide who you are every day. You have the power of the now on your side. You cannot change the past. The past is dead and gone. It does not define you today. Be the person you want to be and know that the Lord is with you.

God is asking you to put aside your life, your world and your needs for a few minutes of your day. Can you do that? Can you devote a few minutes to completely dedicate your mind to Christ and the Holy Spirit?

ONE LIFE...ONE LOVE...ETERNAL

MAY THE SEEDS OF DECEIT BE BLOWN AWAY LIKE CHAFF FROM THE WHEAT

42 TIME

The Lord is with you today. The Lord God is pleased with the work of the daughter. Prayer and meditation bring forth the touch of the Holy Spirit and allows us to speak through the daughter.

Be filled with the power of the love of God. Let it fill every cell and let the body be healed and brought into alignment. Today is forever, if you live in the moment. There is no turning of each moment, the clock is an illusion created by man. There is a time for everything, because the moment is eternal. The moment is now!

When you are unhappy you feel it is forever and time does not pass, in contrast when you are happy you see time flying by. Have you ever been engrossed in a project you love and it took hours of labor but it seemed like it only took a moment? This is because you exist in that moment.

Accept and learn today that time is an illusion. Eat when you are hungry. Sleep when you are tired; learn not to be programmed by the clock. Conform for work and for scheduled events but learn to listen to the body, the heart and the lead of the Holy Spirit!

ONE LIFE...ONE LOVE...ETERNAL

MAY THE SEEDS OF DECEIT BE BLOWN AWAY LIKE CHAFF FROM THE WHEAT

This is why we always say there is a way to do all things. The moment is eternal; the self-imposed deadline is the illusion. All things will be done; all you need to do is make an effort to be organized. Plan and prioritize yourself. Put God's time first, plan what you need to do and see it all falling into place, going perfectly. Your day is like a River. It will flow between the banks unless you allow the rain to fall and cause the flood. You control your life, because you are an individual, one unit and you control what affects you. If a stranger comes up to you and start screaming at you, telling you about their problems, how will that affect you? You didn't cause it and you can't fix it!

You are an island. The winds will blow and the tide might rise but the island sits and waits for the calm. Be an island of calm in the storm. Control the emotions; do not be controlled by mere hormones! Stay God centered and the storms will become fewer and fewer. You attract what you are. What do you want to attain in your life?

Meditation will help you build your God center and give you the peace that you need to carry. Learn to be in the eye of the storm. The world rages all around but the center is calm. Your control comes with the calm! Find your center and

MAY THE SEEDS OF DECEIT BE BLOWN AWAY LIKE CHAFF FROM THE WHEAT

find the peace God sends you. I love you as always.

> *Romans13:11 and that, knowing the time, that now it is high time to awaken out of sleep: for now is our salvation nearer than when we believed.*

ONE LIFE...ONE LOVE...ETERNAL

<u>MAY THE SEEDS OF DECEIT BE BLOWN AWAY LIKE
CHAFF FROM THE WHEAT</u>

43 GUIDES

The Lord is with you. There is a constant battle for the lives of mankind. This is a long fought battle. Man is attracted to disobedience and evil. The enemy loves to lure the unprepared and they end up in trouble. All the lures of the enemy are there to destroy lives.

There is a limit to how much the guides can do to try to keep you safe. You have free will in all things. There would be no value in your obedience if you were forced. Love must be freely given. The light is always shining for you but you must choose the light over darkness.

Pray for guidance, pray for protection and pray for the wisdom to discern what is of God and what a lure into darkness is. Center yourself in God. Surround yourself with your guides every day. Ask yourself where am I going from here? You dictate your future; you dictate your path.

> *St. John 16:13 When the spirit of truth, comes he will guide you into all truth, he will not speak of himself, but whatever he shall*

ONE LIFE...ONE LOVE...ETERNAL

MAY THE SEEDS OF DECEIT BE BLOWN AWAY LIKE CHAFF FROM THE WHEAT

hear, he will speak and he will show you the things to come.

Once you allow the Lord to guide, that is when miracles will begin to happen. No one walks alone but their actions and thoughts select the influence they allow in their lives. The choice is up to each individual. What do you want in your life?

There is some danger in making the wrong decisions. The guides gently lead you, but if you ignore their urging and you stray from the path, that is where the danger lies. Influences await your choice. Every time you tarry and continue in disobedience you place yourself in jeopardy. God loves us so much that he has provided us with our own guides, guardians and teachers, Angels whose sole mission is to help us on our path. Guardian Angels do their utmost to keep us from harm both physically and spiritually. Guiding Angels are there for you to help you navigate through life's challenges and are there to guide you spiritually to help show you the way.

Teachers are there to help you recognize that you are a spiritual being and teach you to use the gifts and talents God has provided for you. We are so

ONE LIFE...ONE LOVE...ETERNAL

MAY THE SEEDS OF DECEIT BE BLOWN AWAY LIKE CHAFF FROM THE WHEAT

loved and taken care of but it is our choice to accept this life. We have free will and we must learn to submit to the will of the creator to walk in the light. You will need to soften the grip on your life and allow yourself to be guided by your higher self and begin to align with the spiritual side of your life.

When we decide to operate from our egos and we begin to live by our own will, then we are assuming the role of God. That is when God steps aside to allow us to walk alone without his guidance and protection. It might grieve him to see you leave, but when you decide to come back he will always be there for you.

- The 1st step of alignment is accepting God into your life and making the commitment
- The 2nd step is making a covenant with God to do his will.
- the 3rd step is receiving the Holy Spirit
- the 4th step is developing the ability to hear the voice of God

Once you come into alignment, your world will begin to change. Know that if you start feeling agitated, nervous or anxious just be aware that that is coming from the spiritual change that is

ONE LIFE...ONE LOVE...ETERNAL

MAY THE SEEDS OF DECEIT BE BLOWN AWAY LIKE CHAFF FROM THE WHEAT

going on within. This is completely natural and not to be concerned about, if anything this is a reassurance that you are going through a spiritual change and are coming into alignment with your spiritual self. Be at peace in the love of the Lord and know that you are loved.

ONE LIFE...ONE LOVE...ETERNAL

MAY THE SEEDS OF DECEIT BE BLOWN AWAY LIKE CHAFF FROM THE WHEAT

44 CALL TO CHRIST

We the workers for Christ call upon the people to come to the light of the Lord Christ Jesus. The workers on the spiritual plain (guides, guardians and teachers) are ready to guide and teach you through the benevolence of the Holy Spirit.

To be a worker for the Lord Jesus Christ your heart must be open and accept the love and guidance of the holy of holies. All who submit to his will to find a love that exceeds the world and all its possessions! Come home to the love of the father of us all who seeks your unity in spirit for the good of all mankind.

Peace unto all who serve the will of the father of us all.

The father of us all wishes us the peace of the universe. To receive the love and wisdom you need all you have to do is put aside the ego (which edges God out), and allow his will to guide you. This world is in desperate need of some help and guidance. Mankind needs to learn how to reach out to God, how to receive his word and how to live in a manner that honors the Lord in all that we do.

ONE LIFE...ONE LOVE...ETERNAL

MAY THE SEEDS OF DECEIT BE BLOWN AWAY LIKE CHAFF FROM THE WHEAT

You can live your life in a normal way. There is no need to assume monks robes or assume a pious attitude towards the rest of the world. All you need to do is follow his commandments to walk in love and compassion. You will attract what you give. Give the world understanding and love so you can reach out and change your world.

When others see the change in you they will become curious and ask what is happening to you. When you explain what you have done and how Christ changed your life, this will make a tremendous impact on their lives. When you begin to give the Lord the glory, your life will glorify him!

The steps to a happier life are so simple:

- Read the word out loud to yourself
- Pray
- Praise and give thanks
- Meditate… Take a moment to stop and listen to the sweet inner voice
- Plan your day with God
- Live your day as planned
- Walk in love and compassion for everyone.

Do these things and you will receive the blessings, favor and guidance from the Father of us all!

ONE LIFE…ONE LOVE…ETERNAL

MAY THE SEEDS OF DECEIT BE BLOWN AWAY LIKE CHAFF FROM THE WHEAT

ONE LIFE...ONE LOVE...ETERNAL

<u>May the seeds of deceit be blown away like chaff from the wheat</u>

45 God's Message

The love of the Lord is with you. Be at peace in the love of the Father of us all. The world is losing its way into darkness. This is an effort of the Father to use the love of one woman to reach out and touch those people who are willing to receive the message of the Lord.

Christ Jesus came to change the minds of man and to help the people see the way of God. Man ignored the message and the way and built a religion. God's religion is love God's message is love. We are to love one another no matter what.

Love does not mean you agree; it just means that all you can do is love. Stand by the words of Christ Jesus; know that all Christ Jesus did you can do also! All the love of God is yours, just as the universe is limitless so is God's love.

God makes the laws that rule the universe and mankind. God has given you dominion and you threw the gift away. God gave you the power of Christ Jesus through His sacrifice and you threw that gift away also. Study the science of the Lords work. Faith, love, compassion and the obedience of Christ Jesus can change your world. When you change your world it affects the person next to

MAY THE SEEDS OF DECEIT BE BLOWN AWAY LIKE CHAFF FROM THE WHEAT

you. It will operate like a chain reaction. Everyone has the power, but all do not accept the responsibility.

Some are lost, attracted to the darkness. The way of darkness is easy. In the darkness anything goes; there are no rules. This path leads to disaster and ruin. It will take you down and it will feed through the family and the generations, growing like a cancer and only the Light of God can kill the cancer of darkness. Purity kills impurity, heals the heart and mind of the infected. Man is drawn to darkness, unless he turns to the Light, but this requires work and obedience.

Don't be easily seduced by the world. Try to see the world through the eyes of God. If you know it's wrong, step away and leave. Never worry about what the world will think; worry what God would think!

Look for a new way. Look for the truth. The truth lies in Christ Jesus. Eliminate the words and works of man and seek the words and works of truth!

ONE LIFE...ONE LOVE...ETERNAL

<u>MAY THE SEEDS OF DECEIT BE BLOWN AWAY LIKE
CHAFF FROM THE WHEAT</u>

46 ELEVATING YOUR LIFE

The love of the Lord is with you. The gifts of the Holy Spirit are many. The love of the Holy Spirit is unimaginable until you arrive at the place of alignment. Once you receive the presence of God you will get a sample of the nature of God's realm. What you do here relates to the experience you will have when you transcend this life for the next.

People have had visions of the heavenly realm, but they only see in metaphor, in a way they can relate to. The mind can only conceive of what it can understand. Most true things of God are not understandable in the human realm. To truly understand and see we must wait until we transcend this life.

The level of evolvement relates to the levels of heaven that John speaks of in the Bible. The only way you will understand is through spiritual communion. This ability is a result of prayer and meditation. When you pray it draws nearer your guiding Angels and the Holy presence.

When you meditate you still the mind and allow the alignment process to flow from the spiritual self to the body. Vibrations affect the state of the meditation and the spiritual self.

ONE LIFE...ONE LOVE...ETERNAL

MAY THE SEEDS OF DECEIT BE BLOWN AWAY LIKE CHAFF FROM THE WHEAT

Meditation on the Holy Spirit elevates the vibrational level of the body and helps to align the two selves into harmony; this opens the door for the Holy Spirit which opens the way for you to receive your spiritual gifts and allow miracles to begin in your life. As you exercise your spiritual muscles you will be able to manifest the things that you need. You cannot manifest things that you do not need. You will receive the gifts at the time God deems them useful. You cannot set the time or the place. Only the Lord knows when and why. All things are for your good. Some are lessons, some are guidance, and some are to show the love of the father of us all holds for you. Be blessed today. Do good works. Keep your mind on the Lord. Be aware of all that you think and do. Stop just doing time and start living.

Seek communion between the Holy Spirit and the waking mind. Train your mind, train your mouth, train your attitude and you will elevate your life.

Be one with the Father of us all.

ONE LIFE...ONE LOVE...ETERNAL

47 FORGIVENESS

The love of the Lord is with you this day. Much has already been said about forgiveness. It is essential that we see how important forgiveness is in our life. Forgiveness allows us to give our problems and our regrets to God and move on. The only way to let go of the past, let go of regret and make progress in our life is to forgive. Men of God are those whose hearts are seeking the truth in their life.

- Never doubt the love of God is in your life.
- Forgiveness is there for all who seek it.
- Forgiveness clears the mind and the spirit.
- Forgiveness is a release of past hurts.
- Forgiveness is an act of love.
- Forgiveness is a godly behavior.

Search your heart. Are you holding onto a hurt that you cannot release? Is this stopping you from moving on in your life? To forgive is not to condone what was done. Many great hurts both physical and emotional or real and they have damaged the heart, the mind and the soul. The past cannot be changed, no matter how much you would like to go back and alter what is happened. The only solution is forgiveness, so the wound can

MAY THE SEEDS OF DECEIT BE BLOWN AWAY LIKE CHAFF FROM THE WHEAT

heal. There is no room for hatred and regret in a heart that is full of love. You must learn to forgive and learn how to live in the present moment.

If you been wounded in the past, that can be much like a poison dart in your heart. The only way that you can heal that heart is to remove the poison dart. Releasing all feelings of hostility, regret or anger is the only way you can heal your heart and begin to be whole again.

If you have wounded someone in the past and the guilt is eating you alive, I want you to know that no matter what you have done you can be forgiven. We have so many people, right now, that are suffering from posttraumatic stress. This causes feelings of guilt, anxiety and fear to resurface when triggered by current events. The heart, the mind and the spirit are all damaged and need to heal. There is a way to heal a heart and to make a person whole again. This requires the person that was hurt to take the experience to God. The event that is haunting you can be given to the Lord. This requires you to humble yourself before the Lord, to tell him what is troubling you, and for you to lay it on the throne of God and allow God to take it.

ONE LIFE...ONE LOVE...ETERNAL

MAY THE SEEDS OF DECEIT BE BLOWN AWAY LIKE CHAFF FROM THE WHEAT

This is the cleansing ritual, because we know that God knows what you're going through. But this act of contrition allows us to give it away. We can't cure the abuse for the pain but we can give it away. What better person to give it to the Lord Christ Jesus who sits upon the throne at the right hand of God awaiting you. God wants you whole. God wants you healed. There is a love beyond description and awaits you, if you will just come take it to the Throne of God. Once you to know how much you are loved today and every day, you will understand how blessed you are. God wants you to be at peace and wants you to know that you are loved, just as you are.

ONE LIFE...ONE LOVE...ETERNAL

MAY THE SEEDS OF DECEIT BE BLOWN AWAY LIKE CHAFF FROM THE WHEAT

48 THE BOUNTY AWAITS

The Lord is with you today being at peace in the love of the father, who loves his children beyond measure. To his children the Lord sends his word.

To love God is the purpose of God's children. Love is the guide to God. Words are just words, must be spoken out of love and devotion. Empty sermons, empty prayers full of only love for the self; do not touch the heart of God. If you want the presence of God's precious Holy Spirit you must put away your selfish pity for yourself and reach out to the father in love.

Pray for what you need, pray for God's will to be done, pray for purpose and guidance and pray for the peace of the Lord to fill your life. All that you need has been prepared and the feast is on the table, all you have to do is join in the banquet. Thank God for your bountiful life, then bless the feast and give thanks. Then sit at my table and eat of the bounty of the Lord and drink of the living water.

The fruit from the tree of life is set before you and all you have to do is get to the table. You must follow the narrow path that God has set before you. You are now walking in the Valley of the

ONE LIFE...ONE LOVE...ETERNAL

MAY THE SEEDS OF DECEIT BE BLOWN AWAY LIKE CHAFF FROM THE WHEAT

shadow. Look for the light from on high and make the climb out of the Valley of darkness and rise to the light.

A Beacon is being put before you, but it must be your choice to choose higher ground. As you climb higher, the air becomes purer, and your heart becomes lighter. The bonds and the chains of the world will fall away and you will find freedom.

Let the Beacon of God's light show you the way. Continue to learn how to live in the light, these are precious lessons sent forth to reach the seekers. One woman has prayed before the altar of the father for this to pass. Do not let this go unappreciated. Follow the lessons and take them to heart and believe there is a living God and he is here to care for the faithful. Be a blessing to the world. Be a messenger of the word. Do not judge others, but offer love!

Be at peace in the Lord

Follow your inner compass and the soft voice that leads from within. Lead the best life you can and stay on the path that God is laid out before you. Waiting for you at the top is the tree of life and beneath the tree God has laid the table full of his bounty which is God's love. Your mission is to

MAY THE SEEDS OF DECEIT BE BLOWN AWAY LIKE CHAFF FROM THE WHEAT

make the climb and accept what God has provided for you.

Standing at the top of the path is a guide, holding a lantern high so you may have a guiding light. The 12 fruits are ripe on the tree and the 12 chairs surround the table and it is all waiting for you, to accept the bounty of God's harvest. All you have to do is assume your position.

It all starts with taking up your lantern, filling it with oil and trimming the wicks of the lantern, so you are ready when the darkness falls. The lantern is God's love, the oil is being spiritually filled and the wick is maintained through prayer and communion with God. This is the quest of every human being that walks the earth. Are you ready to structure climb? Are you ready for the fruits of life? It's up to you to decide what awaits you and how prepared you are to make the climb. Know that you are loved and the quest is being laid before you. You have free will and you have free choice.

ONE LIFE...ONE LOVE...ETERNAL

49 ABUSE

The Lord is with you today. The love of God is your greatest gift. The love of God will set a fire in the land. That is how to see it! The message is the ember of the flame sent forth into the kindling wood that the drought of the Lord in the world has prepared for the message. The wild fire will burn for God. Praise and prayer will light up heaven and the Angels will sing for joy that man loves the creator. The Angels rejoice each time a prayer rises to God.

They weep for the lost who do not know the truth and the way. Keep your heart on God and do the work you dream of. There are many who lost the way because of abuse. Sexual abuse causes a sexual obsession and they cannot release that desire that was awoken before the mind and spirit was ready to guide the balance that was needed. When one abuses a child and that child grows up and abuses the first must answer for the chain of destruction that follows. The cure is within God's power but they make their obsession their God. They refuse to allow God to change their thoughts and deliver them. My husband was very strong to have survived the abuse he suffered as a child both from his adopted mother and from his

MAY THE SEEDS OF DECEIT BE BLOWN AWAY LIKE CHAFF FROM THE WHEAT

biological family through alcohol. He is a walking miracle. He loves the children and awaits the opportunity to protect them from the abusers.

The devil later laid the temptation to continue the cycle of abuse before him when he was a teenager but he turned away from that path and God rejoiced at his strengths. That day he chose the path of God.

Too many do not resist that first temptation and that ruins the rest of their lives. There can be a healing from abuse, but the abuser is lost to the obsession. That is the truth, because God can heal all things but you must want the healing. They don't seek the Lord's help. They are lost in darkness and the adopted mother's father must suffer because of what he did through alcohol. The adopted mother will be answerable for a life of sex. She knew and sought God's absolution each time but she threw away grace each time to return to her old ways.

The giving of absolution is not for a man to stand in place for Christ. Only Christ can give grace because only God sees into the heart. The priest just gives the petitioner a person to voice their sins to, the priest is just an ear while the voice goes up to God. When the priest offers absolution

MAY THE SEEDS OF DECEIT BE BLOWN AWAY LIKE CHAFF FROM THE WHEAT

he is offering the grace of God but in it lays the condition that the petitioner has seen the error of their ways, and is ready to change and to go forth and sin no more. The Priest should not consider themselves a part of Christ, but a worker with Christ.

Much has been lost from Peter's church. Originally it was based on the truth. Money, politics, sex and pride have taken down Peter's work. John is trying to reach out and build a pure message of truth through these writings. There are many who watch over this work and have partnered with the writer. If you allow him, John will guide you in a truth for he sees your heart and knows your desire. May the peace of God be with and you know that you are loved.

ONE LIFE...ONE LOVE...ETERNAL

MAY THE SEEDS OF DECEIT BE BLOWN AWAY LIKE CHAFF FROM THE WHEAT

50 THE SCIENCE OF GOD

The Lord is with you today. We must study the science of the Lords work. All that Christ Jesus did, you too can do. Christ operated through direct communion with his Father. Faith, love, compassion and the obedience of Christ Jesus can change your world. When you change your world, it affects the person's world that is next to you. This can set forth a chain reaction! Everyone has the power but all do not accept the responsibility and the work that is required to operate in the realm of the messianic spirit.

Although man is drawn to darkness he can still make the decision to turn away to strive the light. Don't allow yourself to be easily seduced by the world. Look at the world with the eyes of God and say to yourself what you think God would say if he were present. If you know it is wrong, step away and leave.

Never worry about what others think. Worry about what God would think. Look for a new way; look for the truth. The truth lies in Christ Jesus. Eliminate the works of man and seek the words of

MAY THE SEEDS OF DECEIT BE BLOWN AWAY LIKE CHAFF FROM THE WHEAT

truth; the words of God. The Lord is with you today and sends his love.

ONE LIFE...ONE LOVE...ETERNAL

MAY THE SEEDS OF DECEIT BE BLOWN AWAY LIKE CHAFF FROM THE WHEAT

51 THE WORLD TODAY

God is very upset about the way things are going today. The turmoil in the Middle East just keeps getting worse and more and more people are calling out for destruction. Even the Pope is calling for bloodshed. We as humans see the injustice of the world, we see the beheading of Christians and we see the slaughter of the innocent. All of this is caused by people who call themselves religious but in fact religion has very little to do with it. They have a vision of a one government Middle East and they want to be in control of it. Today is September 6, 2014 and this was written in response of what's going on in the world today.

The Lord is with you today. To be loved is God's greatest gift to you.

There is a strong wind blowing all of the hate, which is being generated. It is hard to see the hatred and a bloodlust that is blowing in the Middle East.

If you allow yourself to be drawn into that, and seek revenge then the blood will flow and America and in the United Kingdom, because this is to be a great war created by the enemy of man. There is no way to fight this war with guns. This is

MAY THE SEEDS OF DECEIT BE BLOWN AWAY LIKE CHAFF FROM THE WHEAT

a war that will be fought against the righteous of every faith. These people hate all that are different from them.

The difference is between the beliefs of these men are not based in God. This is a movement that is based on power and control. They seek to dominate their world. Cut off their funds, the world must condemn them and shun them, if this is to stop. This must come from the other Arab countries first because not one of them can survive without help from others.

This is a great dilemma for governments. They will not seek the solution so we must be prepared for war. Do not allow yourself to be drawn into the hatred and seek blood for retribution because to do so is to put your salvation in jeopardy. God's blessing, God's protection and his grace are reserved for those who follow the mandate of God. I know this will be difficult and you will have to search your heart for the solution but please always remember your salvation is your most precious commodity and know that you are loved today.

ONE LIFE...ONE LOVE...ETERNAL

MAY THE SEEDS OF DECEIT BE BLOWN AWAY LIKE CHAFF FROM THE WHEAT

52 HONORING GOD

The Lord is with you today. Every heart here on God's dimension rejoices at the prayers and work of one woman. Regardless of all the obstacles we place in her way, in order to test her faith, and she still reaches out to God for more of His word.

To set you aside and to allow God to speak is a great thing. To submit to His will and not her own is a great thing. We have asked much of this woman and she keeps saying yes Lord, I will do my best.

Let the world hear the voice of the Father of the universe! There is a lack of dedication to God. The whole world hears its own voice and not the voice of the Father. They kill in their own name not in mine! They sit in judgment in my place, in self-righteousness, but not for me, but to make them superior.

My children you must stop this!!! I will not honor you if you do not honor me. I will not put you first, if I am not first. My protection falls on those who are in my family. You see not all of mankind is in my family. All are welcome but to be mine you will have to be accepted.

ONE LIFE...ONE LOVE...ETERNAL

MAY THE SEEDS OF DECEIT BE BLOWN AWAY LIKE CHAFF FROM THE WHEAT

Acceptance is based on love if you cannot love me above all else then you cannot be accepted. If you cannot love another as yourself, you will not be accepted!

There is a hunger in man that he interprets as ambition, and he tries to fill that hunger with success. Are you never satisfied? Are you never grateful? When will you have enough so that you can rest? There is a way to do all things and keep me at your center.

There is a way through prayer, meditation and submission to God's will that will allow you to live a life of peace and contentment. There is a way to live a life of love. There is a way to succeed in life without worshiping money, cars, houses and prestige. Money is not where the evil lays, in greed lies the evil.

The hate that is growing in the Middle East is going to overflow into the world. They will kill in His name. This will cause the wrath of the enemy to rain down on all of mankind. The government will offer you a solution: first they will try to disarm everyone, in the name of a peaceful solution. Then they will require the chip on everyone, so they can locate the subversive

ONE LIFE...ONE LOVE...ETERNAL

MAY THE SEEDS OF DECEIT BE BLOWN AWAY LIKE CHAFF FROM THE WHEAT

element when they act up. All of this will be offered as a peaceful solution to the terrorists.

This is all mapped out by those who operate in the enemy's Army. They believe they can offer peace under one authority, without God, to live in peace. The peace that they will offer you is for all to be like robots, obeying only the orders of their master, who will sit on the throne above everyone and declare himself God on earth.

The men of today who are professing to be of faith will fall like dominoes when the test is given. They believe because they are under God's Grace, the rapture will be their salvation and they will not be tested. When this does not come their faith will fall.

The Lord knows the heart, the strength and the will of each individual. The strength of your faith must be built up now! You must see the danger! The time of tribulation is upon every person and there cannot be a turning back.

The hearts of man has been turned to stone and the mind rages and cries out for blood. Defiance is the path to ruin! Prayer, meditation and faith are needed to survive the tide of blood that is coming. The purpose of this message is not to frighten you

MAY THE SEEDS OF DECEIT BE BLOWN AWAY LIKE CHAFF FROM THE WHEAT

but to warn you. Survival of this tragic event must be prepared for, you must heart and your heart against the anger and keep God at your center. This is written out of love for you today.

ONE LIFE...ONE LOVE...ETERNAL

MAY THE SEEDS OF DECEIT BE BLOWN AWAY LIKE CHAFF FROM THE WHEAT

53 RELATIONSHIP

To you we send love and blessings. The Lord is with you as always. Count the stars in the night sky. That is how many people need the love and guidance to touch their souls today. The love of God is for all people everywhere. You are not in a category unto yourself. God sees every one of you individually. You may think that you have been abandoned, but you have not!

You are not defined in Heaven by a label you have placed upon yourself. That is just a uniform you have put on your soul for the world. To be loved is everyone's driving force. Love is not based on sex but on the relationship you build. When you allow yourself the opportunity to build a relationship it will grow. It will build deep roots that will keep it grounded throughout the storms of life.

Opening your heart to God and not allowing the slings and arrows of the pious cannot be allowed to cause you to turn your back on God. Do you really believe God would abandon you over one area of your life?

For instance, say you have lived your life caring for others. You have been a healer or a helper to everyone you meet. You have done your very

ONE LIFE...ONE LOVE...ETERNAL

MAY THE SEEDS OF DECEIT BE BLOWN AWAY LIKE CHAFF FROM THE WHEAT

best, but they tell you God has abandoned you because you have had a monogamous relationship with someone for 25 years that is not sanctioned by the pious. Do you honestly believe God is not pleased with that life?

Was this soul to be condemned, but the one that goes to church every Sunday but has sexual affairs, has been cheating and lying in his business and has abandon all of God's rules but is sanctified by the community? To the community this person is a fine example of a good Christian!

God sees each life, knows each heart. If the churchman does not repent to God and a change of heart and mend his ways, how do you think he will fare when he meets God? God is real! When you pass to the next life you will be in a place of absolute love. The light of God shines everywhere. You might say everything is in super HD!

You will be greeted by people who love you and they will welcome you. They will be gathered in anticipation of your arrival. Angels will sing to you. You will feel the love and you will understand all the things that you questioned during your lifetime.

ONE LIFE....ONE LOVE....ETERNAL

MAY THE SEEDS OF DECEIT BE BLOWN AWAY LIKE CHAFF FROM THE WHEAT

You will be drawn to the throne, where the book of life is waiting. This is where your works are recorded. All that you are doing now will be there in the book of life. You will stand face-to-face with Christ. He will see you for who you are not by the label you had in life. You will be stripped clean of all pretenses. You see there is no ego in heaven and you will no longer care about those trivial things which obsess you today. You are a spirit soul and only the spirit matters.

The things that were so important to you in this life are like the morning mist that fades away with the coming of the sun. Bank accounts, houses, cars and all the trappings of life are seen with new eyes.

You will become filled with disappointment and sadness because you see these things for what they were, illusions of the ego that you used to fill the void that should have been filled with God. Everyone has that feeling when they are facing Christ and seeing their life before them. They always say how sorry they were, how much they were misled by the world. They always ask for the Lord to forgive them, they didn't understand, they didn't see and that's the reason that I didn't do

ONE LIFE...ONE LOVE...ETERNAL

MAY THE SEEDS OF DECEIT BE BLOWN AWAY LIKE CHAFF FROM THE WHEAT

what I came here to do. Everyone regrets their missteps and their failures.

Once you cast off the old rags of this life, you will see who you really are and what you came to do. Your life is not some race to be won. Your life is a gift, you choose to come here. You were born at the time and the place for you to achieve the purpose you chose.

The guide to your purpose is your heart. Every second is a gift. This is a difficult concept for people to grasp. They want there to be a religion with the mysteries left for the Pastor to work out. They want a leader to do all the work but that's not the way it works! Leaders are there to guide you. To help you see the truth and to stand with you through the good and the bad.

The greatest sin man can do is kill in God's name. The antichrist who is the enemy of man will use religion, ego and fear to create an army in God's name. This is the express lane to hell! If you create hell on earth you will receive, what you could have created.

The greatest work is love: to love your neighbor as yourself, and to love the dirty, the drug abuser, and the alcoholic to help bring them out of

ONE LIFE...ONE LOVE...ETERNAL

MAY THE SEEDS OF DECEIT BE BLOWN AWAY LIKE CHAFF FROM THE WHEAT

darkness. There is room in heaven for all God's children. Regardless of your label and there are so very many of those. You are not your label and that is an illusion. God understands that in this world there is much hatred, abuse, and discrimination and to use the label is your only way to stand for equality.

Please remember that it is not the definition of you it is only the overcoat you wear over the real you. Regardless of race, color, or sexual preference God loves you and sees you for who you truly are.

Woe unto you if you cast out your child because of their sexual preference. This is a terrible sin! Look at the damage you have done to that precious soul. Hard as it might be for you, there can't be condemnation and judgment. You have to leave that to God!

God's grace is reserved for the repentant heart. If you die with hate in your heart, beware! There is no hate in heaven! What you do, what you believe is all carried over with you. You do not carry your jewelry, your bank balance, etc., you carry only what is in your heart.

ONE LIFE...ONE LOVE...ETERNAL

MAY THE SEEDS OF DECEIT BE BLOWN AWAY LIKE CHAFF FROM THE WHEAT

You will get what you give. You will take what you are! Self-righteous, prejudice, hatred, etc., do you think those things will carry you past the throne and to God's Kingdom? If you hate in the name of God, you had better backup and change that heart! That's not God you're representing.

Nothing grieves God more than people taking a great prophet and turning his works into an instrument of war. Each death is like a virus that is released into the air contaminating all it affects. Like a virus it will run rampant until the infection runs its course until the people are immunized to the effect of the virus.

Hate is the virus, God and only God is a cure. Not one human on earth is completely right. If you think you know it all, then you know nothing. If your way is the only way, then you have lost your way.

This lesson is intended for everyone to take a serious look at their life and their hearts. If this makes you angry or upset you, then you might be convicted of the actions that are described. The only solution is to repent to God and to change your heart and your ways. This is a message intending to save your soul and your life. Know that you are loved today as always.

ONE LIFE...ONE LOVE...ETERNAL

<u>MAY THE SEEDS OF DECEIT BE BLOWN AWAY LIKE
CHAFF FROM THE WHEAT</u>

ONE LIFE...ONE LOVE...ETERNAL

May the seeds of deceit be blown away like chaff from the wheat

54 THE WALK WITH GOD

The Lord is with you today. Many are in the frame of mind that what they have been taught is the complete truth. That God is a mystery not to be understood or touched. The Father of us all is not an angry distant man, sitting on high watching and waiting for failure. We are blessed with a living God that wants to walk with you each and every day.

God designed the Universe and how it works, just as He designed His children so that they could have access to the Father. A good Father is there for His children, in times of trouble but also in times of joy. The Universe is set up for you and most of you refuse to learn to control your actions, control your mind and utilized the abilities you were created for.

Let those with eyes see and those with ears listen and you will see miracles and hear wondrous things.

The Lord God does not want you to return to the Old Testament rules and laws. The Son of Man came to liberate you; to show you the truth, the way and the Light.

ONE LIFE...ONE LOVE...ETERNAL

MAY THE SEEDS OF DECEIT BE BLOWN AWAY LIKE CHAFF FROM THE WHEAT

Look at what Christ did, not even death had dominion, why, because He was alive in communion with the Father. Jesus walked every step with God. Nothing was done that His Father was not consulted. To walk and work as Christ did is to be in constant flow with the Holy Spirit, while seeking guidance, seeking the will of God and acting upon it.

This is not an easy walk. That is why it is written, many are called, but few answer and of those that answer the call even fewer attempt to live the life. The world doesn't want you to walk with God, because the world is a distraction, and you must be able to control your focus. You must decide your own path. You must make your own way.

There is a narrow path that leads to the bountiful life. We will endeavor to show you the way and the truth so that you too may walk in the Light.

What will happen if you hide the Light of God and there is someone that is lost in the darkness and they stumble right past you? You might be their last hope and you let them pass you by. Your responsibility (and mine) is to hold your lantern

ONE LIFE...ONE LOVE...ETERNAL

MAY THE SEEDS OF DECEIT BE BLOWN AWAY LIKE CHAFF FROM THE WHEAT

high, living on higher ground, so they can see the light shining in the wilderness.

The narrow path of God is there and it will lead you to the top of the mountain where the bounty of God is lying in wait.

God's true children represent their Father. God's true children are Him walking on the earth. God's children don't judge, they forgive. They don't condemn, they commend. Representing God is to walk as God would have you walk!

ONE LIFE...ONE LOVE...ETERNAL

MAY THE SEEDS OF DECEIT BE BLOWN AWAY LIKE CHAFF FROM THE WHEAT

55 THE Touch of God

The Lord is with each of you. To love God is your purpose above all else. To commune with God is to complete the person. Most people are living singular life of the ego. All they believe is what they see. All they seek is what they believe.

Know this, you are a spiritual being. The atoms that compose you are a robe wrapped around your spirit.

When you seek God in prayer and meditation you are altering the vibration field of the atomic structure of the body. The touch of the Holy Spirit is the force that harmonizes the 2 bodies (spirit and physical) and brings them together.

This is when your God spark becomes ignited and you become more of a spiritual being. When you become filled and unified; this is when you become born again! Being born again is the physical manifestation of being a spiritual being. This is a basic spiritual principal that eludes those on this spiritual plane of existence.

ONE LIFE...ONE LOVE...ETERNAL

MAY THE SEEDS OF DECEIT BE BLOWN AWAY LIKE CHAFF FROM THE WHEAT

Just as you feed your physical body, you must feed the spiritual body. This comes with many responsibilities. Prayer sends your communication to God and starts a chain reaction and throughout Heaven. All who love you and are connected with you also hear your prayer.

Meditation calms the mind and allows God's touch to be felt. Do not be afraid of the silence. Relaxing and looking into your mind allows God's touch to be felt. There is a peace in that touch that goes beyond explaining. Everything slows, the world becomes the illusion, and the spirit becomes the reality.

Negative emotions cannot survive the touch of God's presence. God is made of love, compassion and peace. You are an immortal being. To tell yourself that your life consists of only the here and now or that life does not survive death is an illusion created to eliminate the need for morality and justice.

If there is no God, if there is no continuance of life then why do we need to worry about living a good life? There will be no need for fairness and justice. Without God there is nothing to live for. The soul exists in the spirit realm, then inhabits the body and upon death the soul returns to God's realm.

ONE LIFE...ONE LOVE...ETERNAL

MAY THE SEEDS OF DECEIT BE BLOWN AWAY LIKE CHAFF FROM THE WHEAT

You are here for such a small amount of time. There is no time to waste!

ONE LIFE...ONE LOVE...ETERNAL

<u>MAY THE SEEDS OF DECEIT BE BLOWN AWAY LIKE CHAFF FROM THE WHEAT</u>

56 CREATION

The love of the Lord is with you today. Love is the greatest gift. No one can survive without love in their lives. People deprived of love as babies grow up to be murders, psychopaths, and sociopaths.

A person who lives cut off from the love of God will perish in the perils of the enemy. It is God's love that keeps you safe. It is up to each individual to seek the love and protection of the Lord.

Be at peace in the arms of the Lord. Know that you are loved. Send your love, your praise and your gratitude up to God and bring down a rain of blessings into your life. Never doubt the love or God's intention for your life.

What you believe is created and happens. You forecast your future and you have created the life you are living today! Your life is dictated by you; the power of creation lies within the mind, the emotions and the tongue. Love and faith is the engine; creation lies within the tools.

If you want change, then you must change. If you want love, you must give love. You get what you give out.

ONE LIFE...ONE LOVE...ETERNAL

MAY THE SEEDS OF DECEIT BE BLOWN AWAY LIKE CHAFF FROM THE WHEAT

ONE LIFE...ONE LOVE...ETERNAL

MAY THE SEEDS OF DECEIT BE BLOWN AWAY LIKE CHAFF FROM THE WHEAT

57 BREAKING OUT

The Lord is with you today. There is a way to do all things. To love God is your mandate. Spending time with God is required to grow in faith and spirit. To be a seeker and a watcher for God requires more than a liking of the idea or the title.

A seeker is one that looks to God for answers. We as representatives of the Father of us all are here to guide and help you fulfill their potential, so you may do the works of God. The will of God must be your first priority!

The will of man is man's ego and only seeks the growth and the profit of every act. Self-centered actions isolate you from God and bring only temporary rewards. The ego feeds the outer (carnal) man and the rewards are in the outer world.

There is another world, a spiritual inner space that is boundless. Growing your spiritual self holds a reward you may hold on throughout all eternity. The ego is a temporary thing that dominates the personality and silences the inner voice.

The enemy uses the egotistical man to dominate everyone around them because theirs is the only

MAY THE SEEDS OF DECEIT BE BLOWN AWAY LIKE CHAFF FROM THE WHEAT

way. They see themselves as the center of their little universe. This allows the enemy to seduce them into addictions and sin sick behavior that further isolates them from their God force. That is why they eventually wind up on their knees at 3 AM calling out to God for help!

You are not designed to live without God in your life. Without God you will be consumed with a hunger for more things, more success, and more sin to fill the void. When people cry out for the meaning of life it is a symptom that their life is empty and meaningless.

Without God you are only half a person; constantly questioning everything and wondering why there is no satisfaction! How do you explain so many rich people who are so miserable and their personal lives are such a disaster, when there are so many happy people, who have so little?

Do you want to be crying in a cold empty mansion or do you want to be dancing for joy because your mansion is being filled with joy and love? The steps to your inner joy might be easy or you might have to battle every step of the way.

ONE LIFE...ONE LOVE...ETERNAL

MAY THE SEEDS OF DECEIT BE BLOWN AWAY LIKE CHAFF FROM THE WHEAT

There are circumstances that hold you in the chains of bondage and most of these things are generational. Too many people believe that all you have to do is say the words and the chains are broken and you will be born again and free.

Just as you can wash dirty laundry but the stains remain. The stains require special treatment and they must be rewashed until every stain is removed.

Generational chains have been passed down through lifetimes and they are embedded into the DNA of the soul. God and only God can remove all the stains and make you whole and remove the stains.

Prayer is required along with your submission for God to wash you clean. You may have spirits attached to you that must be removed. The most common spirit is one of defiance that shows up in the mind and causes you to question everything. The mind looks for logical explanations and must see, touch and hear to believe.

ONE LIFE...ONE LOVE...ETERNAL

58 Being Prepared

The Lord is with you today. The lies of Satan are the voice in your mind at 3AM. The goal of the Enemy is to keep you locked in the past and the imagined danger of the future. If Satan is keeping you in the bondage of the past, or worrying about the future, your present time will be wasted and you will be captured by fear.

Fear keeps you from manifesting your dreams. Fear is in the court of Satan and will strike you like a knife in the heart. Now is the time to begin living. It is time to take the doubt, guilt and regret to Christ and allow the Grace of God to wash you clean. You are forgiven the second you present it to Christ Jesus.

You must forgive yourself and release the past. Christ comes to you each day with the sunrise ready to lead you into a new day. Yesterday was like the morning mist that burns away with the coming of the sun. To fear the new day is to doubt Christ. Allow the love of Father of us all to wash away the doubt and fill you with the peace and knowledge that Christ will lead and protect you, if only you would allow it. Trust in the Lord and face the new challenges of your new life that

MAY THE SEEDS OF DECEIT BE BLOWN AWAY LIKE CHAFF FROM THE WHEAT

is prepared for you. Life is your training ground. Everything that happens is for a purpose.

Everything you endure is preparing you for your future. There is a reason you are here. There is work to be done. How can you do the work that lies ahead if you are not prepared? If you waste your life and you don't do your part then someone else will have to fill the void you have left. When you get to the Throne and face the Akashic record, you will have to face your life, what will you say in your defense? You are now warned that you will have to face your life! What would you rather fear your life on Earth or eternity? You have a choice, you have free will and you have the ability to see what the truth is and what the lies of the common man are. The common man lives for his paycheck and his possessions.

The uncommon man sees the world for what it truly is and he does the best to live a life of truth and love trying to follow the narrow path of Light until the time you can join the Father of us all. Fear, hate, distrust and anger are the tools of Satan to control you. Peace, joy and love are the gifts of a life in the light.

The choice lies before each of us!

ONE LIFE...ONE LOVE...ETERNAL

MAY THE SEEDS OF DECEIT BE BLOWN AWAY LIKE CHAFF FROM THE WHEAT

59 THE Logical Mind

The Lord is with you today. As long as you operate with the logical mind accepting only what you see, touch and hear then, the spirit of defiance will hold you in chains. To break this pattern, you must see, hear and touch through the heart. You must reprogram your mind. Your mind follows what it has seen and what it has learned. The mind is programmed by its environment, by what it has been told and by what you allow in your mind.

You must learn to be the guardian of your soul. The mind believes everything you tell it, by what you say, what you watch and what you read.

Are you allowing others to program you? Are you allowing the world to tell you what to think? Do you believe everything you are told? Words have power and you must learn to use that power to control your world. You see, you have the power to call into being what you need. What should you call forth into your life? Ask yourself, am I thinking for myself or am I following the wrong Sheppard?

ONE LIFE...ONE LOVE...ETERNAL

MAY THE SEEDS OF DECEIT BE BLOWN AWAY LIKE CHAFF FROM THE WHEAT

You are more than the label society has placed upon you.

Just because you are considered African American, or Hispanic, Native American, etc. you do not have to accept the stereotype that is placed upon you. You must be proud of who you are and it is up to you to choose how to live and how to present yourself to the world. Please don't allow todays culture to determine who you are or how you act!

If you are gay, do not allow anyone to convince you that God doesn't love you. Do not make your gender become a focal point of your life. You are more than your gender. All of these teachings are for everyone. Does it really matter what color your skin is or what gender you are? You are so much more than that. You are a treasured child of God! The Universe is yours, if you choose to accept the spiritual principals that are being laid before you.

You are not your parents, you are not your neighborhood, please understand, you are created especially for your purpose. You are perfect for what you are meant to do. If God is for you, who can stand against you? The Devil wants you to feel isolated, hopeless, unloved and alone.

ONE LIFE...ONE LOVE...ETERNAL

MAY THE SEEDS OF DECEIT BE BLOWN AWAY LIKE CHAFF FROM THE WHEAT

The enemy of man is the great deceiver and he uses many people, because he will make a tremendous effort to separate you from God. If you aren't important why would the Devil fight so hard to hold you back and diminish your opinion of yourself?

There are many self-proclaimed spiritual leaders who teach bias and prejudice against others. All of God's children are loved. None of God's children will be turned away, if you are faithful, if you honor God and you are devoted to God's work, then you are a part of God's family. Never allow a preacher to take God away from you. They will have to answer to all the souls they have turned away from the Kingdom of God.

You must discern for yourself, you must guide your life and you are your own spiritual guardian. Know that you are loved. No one is beyond redemption and no one will be cast away that offers themselves up to God. Be at peace in the Lord!

ONE LIFE...ONE LOVE...ETERNAL

MAY THE SEEDS OF DECEIT BE BLOWN AWAY LIKE
CHAFF FROM THE WHEAT

60 A New Day

The Lord is with you today. Beloved child of the Father, come into the love and protection of the Creator of the Universe and give away your concerns to the world, for they are of the world and not the making of God. There is a great need for the world to see the need for God. There is a hunger in mankind that continues to grow. Nothing satisfies, nothing they do brings peace to their mind and they do not value today because tomorrow is always calling.

Tomorrow is an illusion. A new sunrise has programmed them to believe that it is the harbinger of a new day. This life span of flesh is your day! Your tomorrow is when you will meet your maker. What you do with your today, will decide your tomorrow. When tomorrow comes there will be only love and light. There will be no more sorrows of the flesh but only the joy of the spirit will welcome you.

You will reap what you sow. Think on this, do not pass this over lightly. All you do today creates your tomorrow. What you have done, will build

ONE LIFE...ONE LOVE...ETERNAL

MAY THE SEEDS OF DECEIT BE BLOWN AWAY LIKE CHAFF FROM THE WHEAT

your place in the Kingdom of God. Have you done enough to pass the portal? I tell you this, if you do not honor God today, you will not receive the reward at the table of God. The gates will be shut to you and you will not enter!

You might rely on Christ for grace to allow you entry. Grace is given to the children because sin is a learning experience. Once you learn the lesson and leave that sin in the past, you are forgiven, because you will not pass that way again. My children are operating in grace, but the Kingdom is built on works.

What work have you done in the name of the Father? How much of your life is dedicated to honoring God with your love your praise and yourself? Our Father has done all he can do to give you your life. Christ came for you. Christ suffered the humiliation of the world for you. Christ took the whip for you. Christ died on the tree of death so that you might get to the Tree of Life.

When Christ returns to you, it will not be to suffer for you. It will not be to lead you back. When Christ returns to you it will be to reap the harvest and to burn the chaff in order to have the Holy ground on the earth once more.

ONE LIFE...ONE LOVE...ETERNAL

MAY THE SEEDS OF DECEIT BE BLOWN AWAY LIKE CHAFF FROM THE WHEAT

The Guardian will return to earth. The serpent will be cast out along with his minions! Will you be in the harvest of wheat or will you be burned away as chaff? Today is your chance. This life of flesh is your day. If you wait for tomorrow, it will be too late!

Seek God today! Honor God today! Know you are loved and seek God!

The metaphor for the sunflowers is true. The seed is planted; the seedling reaches for the sun, so that it may receive nourishment. The nutrition might come from the water and soil, but its life depends on the sun. The field of sunflowers turns to the morning sunrise and its face follows the sun until the setting. Every day, all day long the blossom seek the sun. This is how you should follow God, keeping the eyes on the will of God.

God needs to be much like the background program that runs your computer. It operates everything you ask, but always operating system is running to keep everything functioning properly. God is the operating system of your life. Access God and receive all that you need.

As they say, garbage in, garbage out! Is that an appropriate statement to describe your life? What

MAY THE SEEDS OF DECEIT BE BLOWN AWAY LIKE CHAFF FROM THE WHEAT

are you putting in your mind? You are the Guardian! The enemy is a virus that will eat up your operating system! This is your day. This is your life! What are you doing with your day? Be at peace and know that you are loved!

ONE LIFE...ONE LOVE...ETERNAL

MAY THE SEEDS OF DECEIT BE BLOWN AWAY LIKE CHAFF FROM THE WHEAT

61 TIME WITH GOD

The Lord is with you today. There is a time for all things. God does not expect His children to abandon their lives and become monks.

To each God sends love, guidance and protection. There is coming a time you are going to need God every step of the way. There are forces at work for the enemy. They have money, resources and Politian's at their beck and call. Never in history has man been more distracted.

There is a hunger for more of everything and your money is buying less and less. The moneychangers that were outside the Temple are now everywhere. Each telling you that to be happy you need their product. Look around you; even your cars are full of distraction! Do you really _need_ all that stuff? You want to provide for your family but what does that mean?

What is more important, providing all that society tells you that you need, or should you be spending time with your family, so you can lead and teach? If you do not lead your family, then there is plenty that would love to lead them down another path. One day you wake up and realize you don't recognize your children and have no idea what

ONE LIFE...ONE LOVE...ETERNAL

MAY THE SEEDS OF DECEIT BE BLOWN AWAY LIKE CHAFF FROM THE WHEAT

they have been doing or who they were doing it with.

There is time to be all things that are important and to do all you need to do.

The key is time management, realizing what's more important and prioritizing your day. Put God 1st, get up a little early and spend that little time with God. God will show you the way. God wants you happy, prosperous and healthy. Let Him lead you and your family down a better path. Through God all things are possible, so rest in the love and peace of the Father of us all. Who knows you and your needs any better? Your Father is waiting for you take that step towards unity.

ONE LIFE...ONE LOVE...ETERNAL

62 GOD'S BOUNTY

The Lord God is with you today. You are a child of the creator and when you diminish your life and live in darkness it grieves your Father. We do not speak of filling the ego with your importance. We just want you to see how wonderful you are and what you could have in your life if you would allow it.

You were created for a purpose and you were made perfectly. Questioning yourself is method of inviting fear into your life. Fear is the killer of dreams. You can do all things that you were created to do. To succeed you must have a direction to go in and God is to be your compass. If you are to set your course and sail on fair seas, then you need to be able to lay a course. Otherwise you will be blown by the wind and you will wind up sailing into rough seas. Alone you cannot see beyond the horizon. Only God can see the future and set your course.

If you are lost in the past and continue to do things the way they have always been done, then my friend, how can you grow? The past has served its purpose. You should learn from it and

MAY THE SEEDS OF DECEIT BE BLOWN AWAY LIKE CHAFF FROM THE WHEAT

move on. You are meant to evolve and grow, not just stay planted in the past.

If you want more of God then you're going to have to put in some effort. If you love someone and you do not make time for them, how will you grow that relationship? If you want a stronger relationship with Christ, then you have to seek Him out, show Him your love and spend some time with Him.

There is so much that that awaits those who find time for God! Miracles occur, doors of opportunity open and you will begin to understand the supernatural plan God has laid out for you. This is much more than 2 hours in a church once a week. This is a lifestyle that follows the path God has laid out before you.

ONE LIFE...ONE LOVE...ETERNAL

MAY THE SEEDS OF DECEIT BE BLOWN AWAY LIKE CHAFF FROM THE WHEAT

WHERE ARE YOU GOING?

Imagine it is a warm summers evening and you are down in a small valley and to your left is a narrow path that is dimly lit so you can follow it easily as it gently winds up the hill. A gently breeze caresses your skin and you realized you are sensing a peace that permeates the very air you breathe. It is as if you are gently being pulled up the path. There is a light glowing up ahead. Standing at the top is a tall man holding up a lantern to guide you. He is smiling at your arrival. He has shoulder length blonde wavy hair and he is wearing a long white robe with a golden belt around his waist with a large key hanging from his belt. He calmly greets you and leads you up to a large tree that is covered with different kinds of fruit.

Under the tree is a large stone table and a marvelous banquet has been prepared just for you with all your favorite foods. In the center of the table is an ornate bowl that holds some of the fruit from the tree. On the table, crystal goblets are full of pure, sparkling clear water. Reach for a drink and be filled with living water. Drink in the health and the peace of eternity. There is no rush;

ONE LIFE...ONE LOVE...ETERNAL

MAY THE SEEDS OF DECEIT BE BLOWN AWAY LIKE CHAFF FROM THE WHEAT

you have all the time in the world. The water warms your heart, cools the throat and washes every cell clean. You are healed and at peace.

The bounty of Christ awaits all who drink of the living water and eat of the bounty of the banquet. Eat and drink your fill. God has provided it all for you. This special place has been created for you. A special Angel, Malachi has been dispatched to guide you. God loves you so much and He wants you to have all you want. All the love, all the peace and the entire universe is yours, if you just reach out for it.

This is your place and I want you to know that at any time you need refilling, just close your eyes and breathe deeply... Take yourself back to the valley and make the walk back. Malachi will be waiting.

You see, the harvest is coming for the believers. The workers for mankind will be rewarded; the workers for the self will be left with what they treasured most, all alone with their self.

I love you all today and I want you to choose for yourself.

ONE LIFE....ONE LOVE...ETERNAL

63 DAMAGES

The Lord is with you today. Today another sweet soul passed into God's realm. Morgan was someone that was so loving and she saw the world with the innocence of a child. When she loved someone it was 100%. Her innocence attracted a dark soul into her life, who used and abused her both mentally and physically. This caused her to withdraw from the world and she suffered soul damage that caused the cancer which eventually took her life.

You see abuse damages the heart and the soul. Once the damage is there, the body goes out of balance and it causes the cells of the body to be damaged and this can cause cancer, heart trouble, depression, etc. That is why you need to calm yourself and do not strike out in anger. Anger damages you as well as the one it is directed to. The emotions are a great tool but they are also a mighty weapon. Know this what you subject others to, is exactly what you are bringing onto yourself.

Forgiveness is the answer to anger. Love is the answer to abuse. This does not mean to allow yourself to be abused, this means you should get

MAY THE SEEDS OF DECEIT BE BLOWN AWAY LIKE CHAFF FROM THE WHEAT

out of the abusive situation, and then you must release the pain by forgiveness. You must put your faith in God to resolve and heal the damage within. Only through forgiveness can you put this pain aside and heal. If you hold onto anger and fear it will destroy you! Anxiety, depression and all the other psychological terminology that there is a prescription for are all related to fear. Fear is the greatest weapon of the enemy.

When fear gets planted into the heart it is like a weed that grows roots that bind the heart and extends to all parts of the mind and the spirit. Much like an obsession that starts with a thought that you hold onto, the thought dominates the mind it moves into the heart and starts to dominate the mind. The person can't let go of this thought, whether it is an act, an idea or another person.

The Devil plants that seed and it grows and grows until it destroys! There is only one cure for this and it comes first from recognizing that this is destroying your life. Then comes prayer to loosen the ties and destroy this hateful thing at the root. Through prayer and desire you can rid yourself of destructive behavior.

ONE LIFE...ONE LOVE...ETERNAL

MAY THE SEEDS OF DECEIT BE BLOWN AWAY LIKE CHAFF FROM THE WHEAT

The problem is, we won't see ourselves for what we are and what we are doing to ourselves. If you weigh 300lbs then there is something eating at you and you are defending yourself with food. If you weigh 80lbs and see yourself fat then something is starving you and you are trying to starve it out of your life. Something has happened to you and you have accepted it as a truth when it is really a lie. The spirit of the lie, binds itself to you, and takes over the mind.

Who you are today, is the accumulation of your life. It is up to you to decide if you are a victim of the past or are you a warrior that is willing to fight to be the person you want to be. There is someone who sees your pain, understands the damage, but sees you in the eyes of your possibilities. You were created for so much more than you are living. We live such little lives. Limiting ourselves to what the world tells us, watching the world through the eyes of television and the internet. Open your eyes to the possibility that you are more, that you are loved and you can be what you are created to be. That is why this is being written! To give you a new hope, to see new possibilities and to embrace who you were created to be. Give yourself a

ONE LIFE...ONE LOVE...ETERNAL

MAY THE SEEDS OF DECEIT BE BLOWN AWAY LIKE CHAFF FROM THE WHEAT

chance at true happiness. Walk away from the old and embrace the new you.

Christ promised if you would accept Him then He could make you a new person, free of the guilt and conviction of the past. He delivers all this and more to all who seek Him, so you can be created into a new being, full of joy and love. Which do you choose?

The repercussions of a wrong decision can't be changed. There is nothing that can't be forgiven, but once the consequences of your actions are put into motion, the die is cast. Once the damage is done, the act is available to God's Grace, but the physical action has begun, because God can't erase the effects of what you set into motion. We need to live in the presence and protection of the Holy Spirit. If we follow the dictates of the Holy Spirit, He will guide you and keep you from straying into the peril of the world. The true nature of God is love. God wants you to walk with Him, talk with Him and stay under His grace and protection.

> ***Romans 12:2** And be not conformed to this world; but be transformed by the renewing of*

MAY THE SEEDS OF DECEIT BE BLOWN AWAY LIKE CHAFF FROM THE WHEAT

your mind, that you may prove is good, acceptable and perfect, the will of God.

64 THE JOURNEY

The Lord is with you today. Know that the love of the workers for Christ Jesus is yours. Those that profess their faith to the world, draws us to them. There is a fellowship between those of us here and the workers for Christ, in your existence.

Don't be confused about the fact that there are multiple existences. The life force is an eternal fact. When you complete this life here and the body fades, the life will end to the eyes of those left behind. There should be no fear, for you see this life is eternal. You will close your eyes as if to sleep and you will awaken here. There will be music, laughter and a great celebration, for a loved one has come home.

Yours is pause in a long journey to understand. God has made you in His image. Your soul is like a chip of the creator. You are a piece of the eternal. You choose to come here to do your work, to learn to see through the illusion of this place and

MAY THE SEEDS OF DECEIT BE BLOWN AWAY LIKE CHAFF FROM THE WHEAT

to be able to see through your heart, and not the eyes.

If you learn this, then all the hysteria of the world becomes like watching a show. Everyone is running around like ants that have lost their way back to the nest. If each person understood the truth of life, there would be no need to steal or kill. The things you all fight for are so irrelevant.

See a man in your mind. He drives a $100,000 car, he wears a coat made of rare animals and he wears a golden watch to clock the days. He takes great pride in his success and he wants to be sure you notice him. He drives by a poor homeless woman, who looks hungry and desperate. She looks him in the eyes, crying because she can't feed her children. He feels all of this in his heart the second he sees her. He looks in her sad crying eyes, with a sneer of disgust, glances at his golden bracelet and moves on.

The woman's eyes follow him as he passes. She came for him, to bring back his humanity and to give him the chance to move outside his pride. You see, no one else sees her! He had a chance and he passed it by. The woman disappears and another soul has failed to see, because we come in different forms to see who you are.

ONE LIFE...ONE LOVE...ETERNAL

MAY THE SEEDS OF DECEIT BE BLOWN AWAY LIKE CHAFF FROM THE WHEAT

Now see a Pastor, he calls himself a man of God. He preaches a sermon of hate and judgment against those who believe different than his followers. Sitting there is a young man that looks to the Pastor for leadership and that seed gets planted. Saturday night he goes out and sees what he believes is an obviously gay man. That seed of judgment grows into self-righteous hate and he beats the man and leaves him in the gutter. Who is responsible for the hurt and the damage? A seed of hate is almost impossible to kill once it takes root in your heart. Self-righteousness, prejudice and judgment are the seeds that lie to you and tell you that you are acting in God's name. These are the tools of Satan! Everyone asks, why does God allow this? It is because God gave dominion of the world to mankind and each has free will.

You must have the tools to discern. If you read the Word and get to Christ Jesus, then you would acquire the ability to discern false teachings and doctrines. God acts through people. We can lead, we can teach and we can come to you. We can give you the opportunity to change, but it is up to each person to choose.

ONE LIFE...ONE LOVE...ETERNAL

MAY THE SEEDS OF DECEIT BE BLOWN AWAY LIKE CHAFF FROM THE WHEAT

You must take responsibility for your actions, see the destruction of the world and understand this is the actions of man not God! You must guard your heart. All are not what they seem.

If we come to your door, will you feed us? Will you give us your coat when we are cold? Who you are depends on what you do, not what you have! God is with you. We are with you. Be at peace.

ONE LIFE...ONE LOVE...ETERNAL

MAY THE SEEDS OF DECEIT BE BLOWN AWAY LIKE CHAFF FROM THE WHEAT

65 STAYING IN GOD ABOVE ALL ELSE.

The Lord is with you today. If every minute of your life is a challenge and you are struggling to stay on your path and you are unable to maintain your joy, then you need to examine what you have been doing. Yours is a life full of potential and love. The fact that most people are unhappy and miserable is a sign they aren't walking in their purpose.

Most of the world has no interest in God's purpose for them. They are too busy trying to fill their life with entertainment. Know this, you are a child of God. You have been given talents, purpose and the ability to succeed. The main problem is most people do not understand what success is! Do you think success is measured in dollars and material things? These things have nothing to do with success.

Success will be measured when you approach the book of life and you are measured for your works for the Kingdom of God. Success resides in your relationship with your creator. Success is loving your neighbor. Success is helping those in need.

ONE LIFE...ONE LOVE...ETERNAL

MAY THE SEEDS OF DECEIT BE BLOWN AWAY LIKE CHAFF FROM THE WHEAT

You don't have to take an oath of poverty. But if you will put love first, the rest will follow. The people you love will not be here forever. Your children are here but for a minute in God's eyes. Your responsibility is to raise your children to know God. Show them what it is like to have a physical relationship with God. This is essential if they are to survive in the coming upheaval. Help your children have a rock solid foundation. They need to know they are loved and understood.

You are not to allow video games to program their minds. A movie is not a babysitter. You must nurture your children, do not rely on a stranger at a daycare center to teach your children. Your biggest enemy is the entertainment industry. They teach your children everything they do not need. They teach our small children that sex is the center of the universe.

Sex was designed as an act of love between two people that love each other and that have committed to be together for life. The relationship must be built on friendship, love and commitment. Once the bond is made and there will be a permanent relationship, then sex is the act that grows the relationship and unifies the couple as one.

ONE LIFE...ONE LOVE...ETERNAL

MAY THE SEEDS OF DECEIT BE BLOWN AWAY LIKE CHAFF FROM THE WHEAT

Love is the key to all relationships. Premature sex can be destructive. If you have a million dollar object and you do not treat it like it's worth a million dollars then it is worthless to you. If you don't treasure something you will throw it away. Not until it is ruined and gone will you see what you had.

It is in the nature of man to never be satisfied, because there is something lacking. The ego will consume you and drag you away from what's important. If you crave (covet) something that doesn't have a pulse you are chasing an illusion. Jealousy will destroy a life, not just a relationship. Envy is a form of jealousy and you can't allow that bitter seed to take root in your heart. RESENTMENT AND HATE

Jealousy and envy are 2 of the enemy's greatest tools. **THEY PLANT THE SEED OF RESENTMENT AND HATE.** Only through God can you remove these terrible destroyers from your heart. You are God's greatest creation! You are loved above all else in the universe. Live your life as a reflection of your Father. This and only this can cure your heart.

Know that you are loved. It is your greatest gift. Window dressing looks good on to the world but

ONE LIFE...ONE LOVE...ETERNAL

MAY THE SEEDS OF DECEIT BE BLOWN AWAY LIKE CHAFF FROM THE WHEAT

it is only on the outside. What matters is what lies within the heart. All that glitters is not gold and all that tastes sweet is not good for you.

ONE LIFE...ONE LOVE...ETERNAL

MAY THE SEEDS OF DECEIT BE BLOWN AWAY LIKE CHAFF FROM THE WHEAT

66 STICKY FINGERS

The Lord is with you today. When you go out into the world and you play around in the Devil's realm, you become contaminated. Each time you step off into that world it becomes easier and the bad seed gets planted. You tell yourself that it's ok, everyone does it and you are just trying to have a life.

It's like touching something sticky and you can't wash it off, because a part of the residue stays no matter what you do. The Enemy wants you to tarry and see how good the other side feels. He will tell you there is nothing wrong with feeling good. It's nobody's business but yours what you do. These are the lies of the Devil and they will destroy marriages and relationships. You will wind up chasing an illusion that he has planted into your heart.

Much like the first experience with cocaine, the addict is always chasing that original high, but with each attempt the brain is being burned out so the hunger for more becomes the obsession. Before you know it, cocaine will become their God

ONE LIFE...ONE LOVE...ETERNAL

MAY THE SEEDS OF DECEIT BE BLOWN AWAY LIKE CHAFF FROM THE WHEAT

and the addict will beg, borrow or steal to get more. Eventually they won't be able to feel anything without more and more of the drug.

The enemy wants you dissatisfied with your life, so you will throw it all away so you will be broken and alone, living in sin and darkness. Las Vegas takes great pride in being sin city, telling you that what happens there, stays there. That is a horrible lie, because sin stains your soul and will have a lingering effect on your life. Anything goes is a lie. What will be going is your salvation, your life and your self-respect. If you stray from the path far enough, it is a difficult road to get your life back! God wants you to be safe. He wants you to live an honorable life. Never forget how much you are loved.

ONE LIFE...ONE LOVE...ETERNAL

67 BREAKING Out of the Ego

The Lord is with you today. There is a way to do all things. To love God is your mandate. Spending time with God is required to grow in faith and spirit. To be a seeker and a watcher for God requires more than a liking of the idea or the title.

A seeker is one that looks to God for answers. We as representatives of the Father of us all are here to guide and help you fulfill your potential, so you my do the works of God. The will of God's must be your first priority!

The will of man is man's ego which only seeks the growth and the profit of every act. Self-centered actions isolate you from God and bring only temporary rewards. The ego feeds the outer (carnal) man and the rewards are in the outer world.

There is another world, a spiritual inner space that is boundless. Growing your spiritual self holds a reward you may hold on throughout all eternity. The ego is a temporary thing that dominates the personality and silences the inner voice.

The enemy uses the egotistical man to dominate everyone around them because theirs is the only

MAY THE SEEDS OF DECEIT BE BLOWN AWAY LIKE CHAFF FROM THE WHEAT

way. They see themselves as the center of their little universe. This allows the enemy to seduce them into addictions and sin sick behavior that further isolates them from their God force. That is why they eventually wind up on their knees at 3 AM calling out to God for help!

You are not designed to live without God in your life. Without God you will be consumed with a hunger for more things, more success, and more sin to fill the void. When people cry out for the meaning of life it is a symptom that their life is empty and meaningless.

Without God you are only half a person; constantly questioning everything and wondering why there is no satisfaction! How do you explain so many rich people who are so miserable and their personal lives are such a disaster, when there are so many happy people, who have so little?

Do you want to be crying in a cold empty mansion, or do you want to be dancing for joy, because your mansion is being filled with joy and love? The steps to your inner joy might be easy or you might have to battle every step of the way.

ONE LIFE...ONE LOVE...ETERNAL

MAY THE SEEDS OF DECEIT BE BLOWN AWAY LIKE CHAFF FROM THE WHEAT

There are circumstances that hold you in the chains of bondage and most of these things are generational (generational chains are family traits that are passed down, such as defiance, addictions and abuse). Too many people believe that all you have to do is say the words and the chains are broken and you will be born again and free, but you need to understand, just as you can wash stained laundry, unless properly treated, the stains remain. The stains require special treatment and they must be rewashed until every stain is removed.

Generational chains have been passed down through lifetimes and they are embedded into the soul. God and only God can remove all the stains and make you whole again, but sometimes the process takes devotion, determination and work.

Prayer is required along with your submission for God to wash you clean. You may have spirits attached to you that must be removed. The most common spirit is one of defiance that shows up in the mind and causes you to question everything. The mind looks for logical explanations and must see, touch and hear to believe. You can't see the energy that resides within the atom, but the

MAY THE SEEDS OF DECEIT BE BLOWN AWAY LIKE CHAFF FROM THE WHEAT

power is there none the less, just so is the power of God in your life.

ONE LIFE...ONE LOVE...ETERNAL

<u>MAY THE SEEDS OF DECEIT BE BLOWN AWAY LIKE
CHAFF FROM THE WHEAT</u>

68 LETTING GO OF THE PAST

The Lord is with you today. We are amazed at the people who claim to be of the faith, but they continue to live a life of anger, hate and retribution. Know this, if you live a life of judgment and retribution, then that is what you call into your life. You get what you give. You reap what you sow.

When someone hurts you and you return that hurt with anger, then the problem will magnify. Blessed is the meek, for they do not shout out to the world their opinions that cause trouble. Blessed is the peacemaker. The one that strives to heal the situation and give what is needed to heal the situation.

Blessings come to those who offer what Christ Jesus taught. No possession is worth fighting for. Things will pass away, but love is eternal. Learn to love everyone for who they are not who you think they should be. You do not know what damage they have suffered in the past. Most anger is a response to pain. Emotional scars are the chips they carry on their shoulder. They look for imagined hurts so they can strike back at the

MAY THE SEEDS OF DECEIT BE BLOWN AWAY LIKE CHAFF FROM THE WHEAT

demons of their past. Compassion is the only answer.

There is a way to heal a heart. The past does not have to rule your life. Trust us when we say this to you, what has passed in your life is gone and what matters is today. Why should you carry the burdens of that which is gone?

You can give it away and find peace. When you give someone a gift, you don't go back every day to visit your gift, do you? It is that simple to give away all that is holds you back to God. It is a simple act to mentally wrap it up in a package. Imagine a box, and place all the hurts and the pain and carefully put in into the box all the pain, all the abuse, all the fear, and make sure it is big enough to hold it all. Tape it shut and wrap it up any way you want to make sure it's secure.

See yourself picking up the box, notice how heavy it is, and just think you have been carrying that around for so long. Now I want you to carry that box up a long isle way to an altar, climb up the steps to the altar and place the box down and walk away. You are leaving all that behind you. It can never hurt you again! This will start the process of healing. Whenever the demons of the past attempts to come back to you, you must say

MAY THE SEEDS OF DECEIT BE BLOWN AWAY LIKE CHAFF FROM THE WHEAT

that is no longer mine, go talk to God about that because I gave it away. It is no longer mine. Let go and let God. Be blessed today. You are loved.

****If you wish, you can literally get a box, write down every hurt, every snub or every mistake and physically place it in the box, then take the contents and burn them. When the smoke rises, see it all going up to God. If you like you can include incense to sweeten the smoke. This can be repeated as many times as needed. ****

ONE LIFE...ONE LOVE...ETERNAL

MAY THE SEEDS OF DECEIT BE BLOWN AWAY LIKE CHAFF FROM THE WHEAT

69 THE COMING DAYS

The Lord is with you today. There is coming a time when you can no longer sit on the fence. You will have to decide if you will stand for the Lord or crawl off into a corner and hope for the best. God will not stand for anyone that will not stand for Him! Too many people just allow things to just go by. No one seems to care for their brother.

This is the time to decide what you will allow in your life. Just as a rose bush must be trimmed back to get the best blooms, you must trim the wild growth from your life. If it is not of God then it must be cut off before the rot sets into the bush. This is one of the most difficult things you will ever do, but it must be done!

> *2 Corinthians 7:14 If my people, which are called by my name, shall humble themselves, pray and seek my face, and turn from their wicked ways; then will I hear from Heaven and I will forgive their sin and I will heal their land.*

ONE LIFE...ONE LOVE...ETERNAL

MAY THE SEEDS OF DECEIT BE BLOWN AWAY LIKE CHAFF FROM THE WHEAT

The enemy of man is everywhere and he is feeding the hate and the insanity of the world. You must learn to discern what is of God and what is not. God does not want His children to be lukewarm. The Lord does not want you to sit in your room, with your bible, surrounded by your family and hide.

> **Revelations 3:15-16 I know your works, that you are neither cold nor hot. I would have that you were either cold or hot. So because you are lukewarm, and neither cold nor hot, will I spew you out of my mouth.** (Paraphrased)

You must be a testimony to God, you must be a worker, a warrior and a watcher. If there was a war on, would you protect your country? Wouldn't you prepare yourself as much as possible? Guess what? We are at war! It is here and it is now! There is a war to stop your faith. To put you into a box labeled fanatic, just as if you were a terrorist. There are terrorist organizations that are being called religious groups. You on the other hand are considered the enemy if you do not follow the dogma of the one world

ONE LIFE...ONE LOVE...ETERNAL

MAY THE SEEDS OF DECEIT BE BLOWN AWAY LIKE CHAFF FROM THE WHEAT

government that comes to you as the peacemaker. They will strip you of your rights and feed you the political lie, that faith is the same as religion. You must see the difference if you are to survive. I am telling you this, because your salvation is at stake, and they will strip you clean and leave you naked at the mercy of the enemy and his puppet government.

Your salvation is your greatest asset and faith is the key to your salvation. You can't walk with Satan and keep your faith in your back pocket. Thinking you are good enough to make it or that you are a spiritual person for instance is not going to get you through. God is all about love but you will have to return that love through worship and faithfulness. There is no gray area where God is concerned. Either you are a worshipper or you aren't! You are going to have to choose, will you walk with God or will you walk with the enemy?

The time is coming, you must choose. There will be no turning to a better time. Mankind has thrown that away. Do you follow your heart? Or do you follow the leader? The life of the flesh will destroy you. The terrorists will not come with bombs, they will come with legislation and they

MAY THE SEEDS OF DECEIT BE BLOWN AWAY LIKE CHAFF FROM THE WHEAT

will lead you by the nose to a promised better life of peace and harmony.

Beware of medications that are coming. They will eliminate anxiety and stress because they will kill the part of the brain that allows you to commune with God. The pineal gland is the center of your emotions and your ability to perceive danger or anger. It is the source of you communion with your higher self and that is your God connection with the Holy Spirit.

Imagine a drug that is cheap, that takes away your will and allows you to be led by the nose because you will be emotionally dead. Your inner voice will be shut down and you will follow for the greater good of the people's state. The people will flock to get it. The effect will be hypnotic to the will and those who take it will be lost.

You must be aware, you must be vigilant if you want to live. God demands this of His children. If you do not stand for God you will fall for a hell on Earth. If this disturbs you, then this is making you think. If you don't think, question and discern you will be lost.

This is not to scare you, it is to warn you, and so you will be aware to the lies that are coming your

MAY THE SEEDS OF DECEIT BE BLOWN AWAY LIKE CHAFF FROM THE WHEAT

way. Only the truth will keep you safe. There is also several micro-chips that are being developed to implant into the brain to make the individual into a super-computer but this will be reserved for the rich inner circle, the chosen ones of the enemy. There is no need to fear all of this, as long as you stay centered in God. God will protect His children and show them the way. Be at peace in the protection of the Lord. You are loved.

ADDENDUM: We here want you to understand because, he that comes to the Lord with more than one face, shall be cast out! You must be of one faith, one dedication and stand fast in the Lord God Holy of Holies!

Who you are at 1AM must be the same person that goes out in the morning sun. Perfection is not the goal, it is faithfulness that is the key to God's heart. Do not call upon the Lord as a beggar, when all seems lost and then when your supplication is answered, you forget your blessing when you return to the world. The alms of God are not to be taken for granted. God's grace cannot suffer hypocrites and manipulators!

ONE LIFE...ONE LOVE...ETERNAL

MAY THE SEEDS OF DECEIT BE BLOWN AWAY LIKE CHAFF FROM THE WHEAT

70 FAITH

The Lord is with you today. Knowing is the key to success. You must know in your heart because that is believing. The fact God faith is not in hoping, it is a matter of knowing! Just as you know the sun will rise tomorrow, know that God is real, that He is the creator of the Universe and that you are dear and precious to Him.

When you say I have faith in the Lord, stop there! Don't add any if, ands or buts after your statement of faith. When you believe, you are setting the picture in your mind and you are starting the creative process. When you say aloud, I know God will guide my works, my actions and my path, this affirms to the mind what your heart believes. The problem starts when the logical mind (the ego), takes these affirmations and begins questioning how this is going to come to pass.

Man starts analyzing and questioning the how and the doubts begin. Then the wishing begins! It is like a beautiful picture has been drawn in chalk and your doubts are like an eraser that destroys your beautiful work! Eventually you will lose sight

MAY THE SEEDS OF DECEIT BE BLOWN AWAY LIKE CHAFF FROM THE WHEAT

of the picture entirely and you are left with a blank wall, where a beautiful vision once was.

Teach yourself to stay positive. See yourself as you want to be, where you want to go and seeing yourself doing what you want to do. Watch things about what you want, read books about people that have succeeded and become the person you want to be.

God is the great master planner and He has given you a vision of who you really are. Not what others have told you they are, but what God intended for you. That's why you have free will and were built with a great master computer. God is the Creator that has given you all the tools you need for what you want. Your mind is a programmable computer, but you must put in the proper info to get out what you want.

In the cosmic plain there is a master file of information. You are equipped with everything you need to access this library of information and revelation. Focused intention on a problem will get results.

Some of the most successful people get their inspiration from focused intentional meditation. They look at the problem from every conceivable

MAY THE SEEDS OF DECEIT BE BLOWN AWAY LIKE CHAFF FROM THE WHEAT

angle, then they put the question to the universe. They clear their mind, allow all the information to be processed and wait for Devine inspiration to come. If the answers do not come, they set it aside and start something that will distract them. They don't worry or fret, they just wait and soon the inspiration arrives and the problem is solved. It might be an idea or the right person might show up to give you a word or a hand. Even Albert Einstein employed this method when he was researching how the universe worked.

Whatever it is, God has the answer. God knows the way, but the problem is mankind does not want the help of God. They would rather put their faith in other peoples' hands. If they get sick, they fret and worry, which makes them sicker. They allow doctors to fill them with chemicals that are worse than the disease. Doctors are fine, but your faith needs to be with God. Your mind controls your body chemistry. Anger, worry and negativity will destroy your immune system and destroy your body's ability to heal itself.

Prayer connects you with a higher power, the Holy Spirit. Gratitude and praise brings forth brings God's presence to you and meditation allows the

ONE LIFE...ONE LOVE...ETERNAL

MAY THE SEEDS OF DECEIT BE BLOWN AWAY LIKE CHAFF FROM THE WHEAT

healing power of the Holy Spirit to flow through you like healing water.

All that you need is waiting for you to reach out and take it. If you were hungry and there was a fruit tree in your back yard, wouldn't you reach out and pick yourself some fruit? The fruits of God's bounty are there for you. Healing living water awaits you! If you owned a mansion, would you live in the cold, dark basement? Wouldn't you climb the stairs and live in the big, beautiful home?

God wants you to be blessed. He loved you so much He came to show us how to live and what was possible. Christ walked on Earth for you! His works were for you! He suffered for you! He died for the sins of man. He tore the veil of separation and sent you His Holy Spirit.

Today's churches do not teach this, they tell you how sin is the killer of the spirit and that miracles don't happen anymore. They want to take God away from the people so they can become their God. They withhold the truth that God is alive, He lives in you and all God that God has is yours. Abundance, health and joy is meant for you.

ONE LIFE...ONE LOVE...ETERNAL

MAY THE SEEDS OF DECEIT BE BLOWN AWAY LIKE CHAFF FROM THE WHEAT

Please wake up to who you are and see the world for what it is! God gave you paradise, God gave you dominion and the power to do His works. What are you doing with your power? What are you doing to build your kingdom?

God is reaching out to you. It grieves Him to see lives wasted on drugs, alcohol and just plain blindness. You are alive, so why aren't you living? Why aren't you doing something that glorifies your life? Wake up and live. Find your joy, laugh a little and you will find your life. You are loved beyond measure. You are a precious jewel to God. He wants you to shine!

ONE LIFE...ONE LOVE...ETERNAL

71 THE STEPS

The Lord is with you today. To me the fact that God leads my steps is completely natural. To others it seems like something supernatural. We here are working to show the world through just one woman what is possible.

The fact that the people in general have not come to the point where they can see. The general public is so blind to the natural relationship with their Creator. There is no answer to the where or the how they became so lost from the natural touch of God. They are empty vessels, walking around looking for something to satisfy a need that can't be filled by the world of entertainment and things. They don't want to commit, they don't want to have to think and they want everything to be instant and easy.

No matter how good the show was, when they get home, they return to the state of emptiness. Satisfaction comes from being filled by the Creator. A path of success is being led by God, which fills the heart and satisfies the inner spirit. Finding God is not hard. Submitting to God's will seems to be the stumbling block. Understand this, Satan wants you to believe you don't need to

MAY THE SEEDS OF DECEIT BE BLOWN AWAY LIKE CHAFF FROM THE WHEAT

submit yourself to anything or anyone. The lie is you can handle whatever happens on your own. The lies of the enemy work best through the hubris and the ego of mankind.

There is a peace in drinking the living spirit and allowing the alterations that are needed to eliminate the chains of bondage that the world has placed upon you. There is a peace in the knowing that you are a child of the Most High God.

Think on this. A child is raised in an orphanage, without love and has never experienced love in his life. He has no concept of what that experience is supposed to be, then he is adopted into a family and is shown love and affection. This is so alien to him, that he fights this new concept. There is a choice the child must make, to accept the love and care of his new family or to remain angry and isolated. Sometimes it takes years to get through the walls of isolation and hurt. How do you prove that love exists, if you have never experienced it?

That is the common man. Society has fed them a lie and they think it is normal, when it goes against the very idea God had for them since the beginning of creation. When they see a person who speaks of God's guidance, His peace and His

MAY THE SEEDS OF DECEIT BE BLOWN AWAY LIKE CHAFF FROM THE WHEAT

love. They begin to react like the abandoned child.

The concept of unconditional love at the cost of surrendering their ego and giving up the bill of goods the enemy has sold them makes them angry and rebellious. After all they are just trying to have a life! They are engaged in a struggle with death, surrounded by darkness and they consistently refuse the Light.

God's purpose is to bring them to the point where they cry out to God because they find their dreams are made of clay. When they get tired of running, that's when they seek the stillness and peace of God. Don't be like the dog at war with its tail. Running in circles and getting nothing for his efforts. Learn to be still in the silence. God is waiting for you to come and find the love you never had. Why live in isolation in an orphanage of the world, when there is a love unending and a home waiting for you.

Seek peace and find God. God lives between the ego and the heart of your soul. Eternity exists, if you will just sit still and see revelation. Know that you are loved beyond your comprehension. Peace resides in the Lord of all creation.

ONE LIFE...ONE LOVE...ETERNAL

MAY THE SEEDS OF DECEIT BE BLOWN AWAY LIKE CHAFF FROM THE WHEAT

It takes time to get to know someone. Take time to get to know your Father, the Father of us all.

Be at peace and know you are loved. You are never truly alone. Your guides, guardians and teachers are always with you, waiting for you to reach out to them. God supplies all you need for every step up the narrow path to His bounty. The tree of life awaits all who see His path.

> ***Revelations 2:7** He that hath an ear let him hear what the spirit said unto the churches; to him that overcomes will I give to eat of the Tree of Life, which is in the midst of the paradise of God.*

ONE LIFE...ONE LOVE...ETERNAL

MAY THE SEEDS OF DECEIT BE BLOWN AWAY LIKE CHAFF FROM THE WHEAT

72 PATIENCE

The Lord is with you today. Know that you are loved. There is a need and a void in people's lives. They are not satisfied with that life. To me there is no other life but I have to remember how long I struggled to find my center. I need to learn to be patient with the world. There are so many people that are as lost as I was. I remember feeling so isolated and alone, crying out to God for help. I had to wrestle Satan and his demons to get free of his hold on me.

I had to struggle for years to eliminate the hold that had been on my family for generations, I was like Jacob wrestling the Angel of God for his blessing. If you have been struggling like I was, it's going to take time to separate yourself from the hold of the past. The demons of the past plant tentacles in your spirit and hold on for dear life. It might be an addiction or a spirit of defiance that holds you back. As you begin to know your Father and develop your relationship you will gain more and more strength. You will have to pray for release and for a cleansing of the spirit. The pure white of God is the most powerful cure in the Universe. The Light of God will clear out all the stain and guilt of the past. The hold on your life

ONE LIFE...ONE LOVE...ETERNAL

MAY THE SEEDS OF DECEIT BE BLOWN AWAY LIKE CHAFF FROM THE WHEAT

can be broken and you can make intentional changes. Here is a joy in being in alignment with God. All you have to do is open your heart to your Creator and ask for help.

I was alone. I didn't know what to do to find God and change my life. That's why I am here, because I don't want you to wrestle with your demons for decades. I love you all and I want you to be free.

ONE LIFE...ONE LOVE...ETERNAL

MAY THE SEEDS OF DECEIT BE BLOWN AWAY LIKE CHAFF FROM THE WHEAT

73 WILL YOU STAND?

The Lord is with you today. How many of you will stand for the Lord when the test comes? The day will come when your faith will be tested. If you do not have a foundation of faith that is set on bedrock, then the Enemy of man will send his minions to test you. Just as the Devil went against Job to prove the weakness of Job's faith, the enemy will try to prove you will fold and fall into the ways of the world.

There is a coming of a great falling away of the unfaithful that profess to be the great workers for Christ Jesus. Just as long as they can profit from carrying the banner of faith, they will profess to be a leader. When the great tribulation starts they will fall like a house built on sand. The wind will rise and the tides will wash away their foundation and they will wash away with the currents.

The people who sit in church every Sunday and listen to the sermon while they plan their week will be washed away. The ones that go to church for the connections and to appear as community leaders will fall away when it is no longer profitable.

ONE LIFE...ONE LOVE...ETERNAL

MAY THE SEEDS OF DECEIT BE BLOWN AWAY LIKE CHAFF FROM THE WHEAT

Who you are is not how the world sees you. Who you are is not what you think you represent. You are what lies in the heart. God knows the truth, He sees the hypocrite, the liar and the cheat. God knows your true feelings and you can't hide from the hand of God.

God does not punish you for your sins. The enemy is the deceiver and the punisher, so he can show the Lord that you are not worth his time and effort. When you wallow in the pit of the enemy, you leave the protection and covering of God. That is when you wind up in despair and find yourself crying out to God. Talk is cheap! You can't talk your way out the pit. To get back to God, you will have to have a broken, sincere heart.

Here is the question, when the enemy puts the test before you, will you stand? When they take you to the center of town and stand you before the masses, will you stand for Christ? Will you be ready? I'm not saying you won't be afraid, but will you stand anyway. Your strength will come from the anointing of the Holy Spirit. That's where your courage will come from. That's where the words will come from. You will have to stand for the

MAY THE SEEDS OF DECEIT BE BLOWN AWAY LIKE CHAFF FROM THE WHEAT

Lord or you will fall into the pit and there won't come another chance.

The tribulation will be the last test, because the trial of faith is final. When Christ returns He won't be the Prince of Peace, because the Lion of Judah will be the judge of the spirit, the heart and your faith. Will you stand with Christ or will you crawl away, back into the darkness and hide? I know this is harsh, you are taught Christ is the Great Redeemer and all you have to do is say the words and you are under Grace. Your Salvation is your greatest treasure and you must keep it Holy. Grace comes to the faithful, which do their best to follow the teachings of Christ and try their best to live the life of a Christian. Grace is not a get out of hell free card. Once saved, always saved is a lie. Each time you fall you must come back and recognize what you have done and sincerely want to change.

Know this, you are loved and Christ wants you to be with Him, but it's your decision, whether you stand or fall. As it is written, so shall it come to pass!

Matthew 24:21-24   for then there shall be a great tribulation,

ONE LIFE...ONE LOVE...ETERNAL

MAY THE SEEDS OF DECEIT BE BLOWN AWAY LIKE CHAFF FROM THE WHEAT

such as was not since the beginning of the world to this time, nor shall ever shall be. Except that those days should be shortened, there should be no flesh that would be saved: but for the elect's sake, those days will be shortened. Then if any man should say unto you lo, this is Christ or there; believe it not. For there shall arise false Christ's and false prophets and they will show you great wonders. Insomuch they will deceive the very elect.

ONE LIFE...ONE LOVE...ETERNAL

MAY THE SEEDS OF DECEIT BE BLOWN AWAY LIKE CHAFF FROM THE WHEAT

74 CALLING ON GOD FOR CHANGE

The Lord is with you today. Love is the key to worship. Love draws the love of God into your heart. There is a great lesson here, if you choose to hear and accept it. If you truly want to draw the presence of God, you must empty your mind of the world and start telling God how much you love Him. Worship is nothing more than showing God you love Him.

Praise is your mouth speaking your heart. Worship is the emotion, praise is the words and God will do the rest! Prayer is nothing more than your communication with God. You don't need fancy rituals, just talk to your best friend, the one that will never forsake you.

If you are lost, let God be your compass. If you are depressed, let God lift you up. If you are soul sick, let God heal you. God is always there for you, but you have to call His presence into your life. Joy comes to the one that calls forth the Lord, just to say I love you. Love can burn away the darkness and despair. Love is the Light of the universe. Love is the greatest gift you can give. Love is the greatest gift you can receive

ONE LIFE...ONE LOVE...ETERNAL

MAY THE SEEDS OF DECEIT BE BLOWN AWAY LIKE CHAFF FROM THE WHEAT

The people of the world make too little of love. They think it's all about romance and they have confused love with sex. They diminish the word instead of honoring it for what it is, the greatest power in the universe. The power of God is based on love. Faith is based on a belief in God and that God's Mercy and Grace are yours because of God's love.

There's a movement to denigrate the people of faith. If you have faith then you are a superstitious moron and a Judas to the real world. Judas said the right things, he played both sides of the faith game. He complied with the Pharisees and the radical Jews all the while he walked with Christ. Judas played the angles, trying to be where the most advantage was for his personal gain. Judas wanted power and fame. He believed in Christ, but he did not understand that no matter what he did, God's plan could not be changed.

Just as you can't change God's plan for the world. You cannot comply with the movers in government who want you to be shamed into throwing away your Bibles and closing down the houses of worship so you can walk in alignment with their ideals. There will be a great falling

ONE LIFE...ONE LOVE...ETERNAL

MAY THE SEEDS OF DECEIT BE BLOWN AWAY LIKE CHAFF FROM THE WHEAT

away from God. Those who do not have a deep seated faith will be blown away like chaff from the wheat. Only the true believers will stand for God. The others will follow the gold to their dream.

Be one with God. Stand unified together and do the works of God. Study and understand the teachings of Christ Jesus. Accept the Christ Spirit into your life and watch as Christ works miracles on you.

- You will learn to walk.
- You will begin to see with new eyes.
- You will be healed.
- You will be resurrected into a new life.

> 1 John 4: 7-11 Beloved, let us love one another: for love is of God and everyone that loves is born of God and knows God. He that loves not, knows God not, for God is love. In this was manifested the love of God towards us, because God sent His only begotten Son to be the propitiation of our sins. Beloved, if God so loved the world, we ought to love one another.

ONE LIFE...ONE LOVE...ETERNAL

MAY THE SEEDS OF DECEIT BE BLOWN AWAY LIKE CHAFF FROM THE WHEAT

75 THE HAND OF GOD

The Lord is with you today. Meditation on God's will is essential. Know this if you think you know what God has planned for you, then you are on the wrong path. God see's things from the end back to the beginning. He knows the challenges you will face and He knows the tests you will have to endure. The intention of God is not known by anyone. You must receive your guidance from revelation and guidance from God. This might not have anything to do with what you have always wanted, because most of that stems from the ego and the programming we received as a child.

God has given us the hand of God to wield, if we choose to accept the mantle of Christ into our hearts.

THE HAND OF GOD CONSISTS OF:
1. ***PRAYER WHICH OPENS THE PATH TO OUR SPIRIT***
2. ***PRAISE WHICH DRAWS GOD'S PRESENCE***
3. ***EMOTIONS... THE POSITIVE EMOTIONS CREATE AND THE NEGATIVE DESTROY***
4. ***VOICE... CALLS ALL INTO BEING FOR GOOD OR BAD***
5. ***MEDITATION WHICH ALLOWS US TO QUIET THE MIND***

ONE LIFE...ONE LOVE...ETERNAL

MAY THE SEEDS OF DECEIT BE BLOWN AWAY LIKE CHAFF FROM THE WHEAT

From now on you must start to follow our directions and begin to pray, praise, worship, meditate and speak your intent. These are the tools of growth. This is the narrow path that we speak of that leads you to God's presence. If you choose to follow the narrow path that leads to a Godly life, then you are called to do these things and make them a part of your daily life. Not only are you mandated to do these things, but you are also called upon to teach and lead others the way.

These 5 practices are your tools and to all who follow the path will receive the filling of the Holy Spirit which is the giver of the gifts of God. The gifts of prophecy, discernment and healing are but 3 of the blessings that will be yours. You will begin to hear the inner voice of God in all aspects of your life. Your inner compass will become fine-tuned and your intuition will grow stronger. This is the way to grow your skills as you grow in faith. Your faith is the foundation on which all else resides.

What a revelation to all who will accept the fact that with faithfulness to the God process, you can build up your spiritual muscles. If you have always wanted a closer relationship with the Lord, this is

MAY THE SEEDS OF DECEIT BE BLOWN AWAY LIKE CHAFF FROM THE WHEAT

how you will make it happen. Society programs you to expect instant results and gratification but this will require work and dedication. I say to you know there is a bounty that awaits all who pursue God with all their hearts.

All things worth doing requires dedication and practice. You must prove to God you are worth spending time with. A life lived hand in hand with God is worth any price, but this costs you nothing but your time and faithfulness. Do you remember trying to lift a heavy box? Try as you might you couldn't lift it alone. You had to get someone to help you lift the box and carry it to its destination. When there is 2 of you, the load gets lighter and you are able to get the job done.

This is what we are teaching. You can't do this alone! You need to partner with God to fulfill your purpose for God's kingdom. You also need to have brothers and sisters in faith to work with you. You need someone who will lift you up and encourage you.

You will not be able to grow in Christ and keep your old life. You will have to look at where you want to go, examine the things in your life and discern what is holding you back. If there are branches in your tree that are not producing fruit,

MAY THE SEEDS OF DECEIT BE BLOWN AWAY LIKE CHAFF FROM THE WHEAT

you will have to trim off the dead wood. Once you begin a God centered life, it will become obvious what is limiting your progress. Chances are, the things you thought made up your life, was not really living. Think of it this way, when you were a child, you loved childish things, but as you grew up your tastes changed.

You can't spend your life riding a bicycle with training wheels, eventually you gain your balance and those extra wheels will slow you down. There comes a time when you must clear away all that is holding you back. This covers habits, people and how you think. The limiting doubts and negativity must be trimmed away. Past guilt's and regrets must be given away and left behind. If you have people who are constantly trying to hold you back, you will have to let them go.

We do not speak of a holier than thou attitude, we speak of a Godly life full of love and compassion. You can't afford to allow the world to clutter you down with excessive garbage! Take a few minutes to sit down and write what you want. List anything that brings you joy and peace. This is listing your blessings, what you want and where you want to go. You are outlining your future. Work on this until your vision is complete.

ONE LIFE...ONE LOVE...ETERNAL

MAY THE SEEDS OF DECEIT BE BLOWN AWAY LIKE CHAFF FROM THE WHEAT

Now make another list of everything in your life that steals your joy and limits you. This includes the people in your life.

This exercise will give you a clearer picture of what is holding you back. So you can start to trim away the dead wood and allow yourself some new growth. Make a decision and a plan to fix what hinders you so you can eliminate the distractions. On the surface this seems simple but it will give you a new vision for your evolving life.

Once you accept Christ into your life you will begin a gradual change within that will alter how you see and feel about things. You will begin to see with new eyes. Make your life list and put it away for a few months, then take it out and read it over. You will be surprised at the changes you will have naturally made once you saw it from a clear perspective. Every year repeat the process and compare the list with the previous year. You will see things with a new perspective, because you must be vigilant and be aware of what is happening in the world around you.

Christ came to make the blind see. Christ came to heal. Will you allow Christ to remove the veil from your eyes? Will you allow Christ to heal your heart? If you don't open your heart to Christ and

ONE LIFE...ONE LOVE...ETERNAL

MAY THE SEEDS OF DECEIT BE BLOWN AWAY LIKE CHAFF FROM THE WHEAT

invite Him in, He can't work in you. Not until you see the need and understand you need help, will you understand that this mediocre life just isn't enough. You have to want more that what you have, because you were created to be more than a worker drone that exists for the hive to survive.

You are a child of God, so live your life like you are special. You are blessed and you have a job to do. It all comes down to free will. What do you choose to be? God is calling all His children to wake up, rise up and claim their inheritance. Be at peace. The Lord is with you on this magnificent journey.

> *Ephesians 1: 17-19   That the God of our Lord Jesus Christ, the Father of glory, may give unto you the spirit of revelation in the knowledge of him: the eyes of your understanding being enlightened. That you may know what the hope of his calling, and what the riches of his inheritance in the saints, and what is the exceeding greatness of his power, which is wrought in Christ*

ONE LIFE...ONE LOVE...ETERNAL

<u>May the seeds of deceit be blown away like chaff from the wheat</u>

76 The Cycle of Life

The Lord is with you today. The Love of God is yours. Each individual is a being with free will, but all are connected through spirit. The spirit of Creation flows through every living being. It is the life force of the universe.

The plan God laid out for the universe is consistent. That is why the Tree of Life is the symbol of the God force. When you grow a garden, the soil must be prepared and then the seed is planted. The seed then grows and produces fruit.

The Tree of Life exists within in the woman, the placenta is a direct image of the Tree, which provides for the child. The living water of life houses the child and it breathes the living water for 9 months. When the living water flows, a new life follows into the world. The placenta follows because it has completed its purpose. It should not be a surprise that so much medical information is held in the placenta, it is the root of creating life.

God's Tree of Life exists for the person that seeks its shade. There is living water for you to drink. The living water is God's love. God is at the center

ONE LIFE...ONE LOVE...ETERNAL

MAY THE SEEDS OF DECEIT BE BLOWN AWAY LIKE CHAFF FROM THE WHEAT

of your being. It is implanted as a spark deep within your DNA. It will lie dormant until you decide to awaken the spark. God will breathe on the spark and it will begin to flicker and grow into a flame.

The Holy Spirit is the conveyer of all you seek. This is God's Spirit that was sent forth to the world to provide for you. You are meant to be protected, guided and loved. Love is the key. The problem is that the world has forgotten what love really is.

Love is not dictated by hormones. Love is not just to be received, but it must be given. Much like breathing, when you inhale you must exhale. When you are filled with love, you must give it out for the cycle to grow and flourish. Much like a flowing river, as it comes to you, it must flow out on others for it to grow. It is not to be reserved for certain people. The love must flow across the land for it to flourish.

When you give out what you need, that triggers a cycle that brings it back to you. Have you ever met a rich person that is so self-absorbed in what they need and deserve that they are never satisfied? They are miserable and they make everyone miserable that must be around them.

ONE LIFE...ONE LOVE...ETERNAL

MAY THE SEEDS OF DECEIT BE BLOWN AWAY LIKE CHAFF FROM THE WHEAT

Then you see the average family that is just making enough to get by, but they are happy and full of joy. Helping anyone to who is in need. Raising their family and loving their life.

Who is the bigger success? What is the secret to happiness? What is the meaning of life? People keep asking this question and the answers are right there when you hold a new born baby. The secret to life is love. Your walk in love and feel like dancing just because the sun is shining or because the rain is falling. The secret is joy for the opportunity to be alive and loving!

Money is not the goal of life, but it's not your enemy either. Money is a thing, a tool for you to use, not a God that owns you. You must know that if you worship money or things you are offending God. The ONLY one worthy of your worship and praise is God. The Father of us all, Christ Jesus and His Holy Spirit are the three that are the one God.

Everything in life is a cycle. Everything must flow for a happy productive life. Just as a tree is pruned back and the dead and unproductive branches are cut off, you must prune your life. If you have dead wood around you, it is essential you cut it away and leave the good productive

ONE LIFE...ONE LOVE...ETERNAL

MAY THE SEEDS OF DECEIT BE BLOWN AWAY LIKE CHAFF FROM THE WHEAT

parts to flourish. Your works go with you, not the things the world treasures so much. Think on these things. Don't allow the goals you have set to distract you from what is important. There is time for all things and if you put God first and your family next, God will bless your works and all that you need will follow.

Keep your eyes fixed on God. You are not how you feel, you are a part of God. Be at peace and have faith. You are loved.

> *Revelations 2:7 He that has an ear, let him hear what the spirit says to the churches; to him that overcomes will I give to eat of the Tree of Life, which is in the midst of the paradise of God.*

**** The churches are the people not the buildings****

ONE LIFE...ONE LOVE...ETERNAL

<u>MAY THE SEEDS OF DECEIT BE BLOWN AWAY LIKE CHAFF FROM THE WHEAT</u>

77 THE ONCOLOGY WARD

*** 10/28/14. This was written when I was sitting with my niece in the hospital. The hospital was full, so she was put on the oncology floor for her gall bladder surgery. As she slept God spoke this word to me. I was hesitant to include this but I said I would relate what God speaks to me....so here it is! ****

There is so much despair here! There are people here that have lost their hope. Know this, this life is a drop in your existence. Everything will pass, but it is up to each individual to decide what they want. To fight for every minute of this existence or to lay the groundwork for the soul.

What they see is not life. What they see is not going to make them happy. This is a deep understanding that exceeds the natural. This is a supernatural philosophy that can only be understood by the intercession of the Holy Spirit. This understanding was historically reserved for the saints and mystics. This was not because they were set aside as special, but because they were the only ones that reached out to God for understanding of the reality of our existence.

ONE LIFE...ONE LOVE...ETERNAL

MAY THE SEEDS OF DECEIT BE BLOWN AWAY LIKE CHAFF FROM THE WHEAT

Once you grasp this concept and it takes root in the heart, life becomes an adventure because the things that were once so important, are now seen as an illusion. The expression, the truth will set you free, is all about the revelation of your life. The decision comes when you decide what the truth really is.

The realization does not come easy. The ego wants to control the mind. Only through humbling ourselves can we diminish the ego and find our life. Everyone talks about what they deserve, what they want and they honestly think these things will buy happiness. Ask these people on this floor and their families how important these things are, when they are living in a hospital room fighting for each breath. Families praying for one more day.

Somewhere on that floor was a man that had never built up his kingdom. He had no fruits of his life to present to Christ Jesus when he arrived at the throne. His name was not written in the book of life. He was in so much turmoil, fear saturated his every thought. His race was over and what did he win?

ONE LIFE...ONE LOVE...ETERNAL

78 GOD

The Lord is with you. Many people question the teachings of the church. They wonder why if God performed miracles and talked to the faithful, then why do they feel nothing when they go to church? They feel as empty as when they walked through the door. Why can't they feel the presence of God in their life?

They must understand the people in the Bible led much simpler lives and they relied on God for guidance and survival. Today there are very few on Earth who are devoted to their creator.

There is so much pollution in the average man's mind and spirit. The body is a well-designed machine that requires balance. Chemicals cause an imbalance. You are filled with chemicals from the water you drink, the food you eat and almost everything you eat is full of preservatives and flavor enhancers. Now they are genetically engineering your grains, fruits and vegetables. Man is no longer satisfied with God's creations, so they are constantly altering to make it "better"!

The world is so busy that it is always distracted. The average human has an attention span of 5 minutes. If you want to see the face of God and

MAY THE SEEDS OF DECEIT BE BLOWN AWAY LIKE CHAFF FROM THE WHEAT

hear His voice, you are going to have to find a way to live a simple life. You are going to have to get back to the basics of a good life.

A good life consists of prayer, faithfulness, eating properly and monitoring how you spend your time. Your day can't be all work to the point you need drugs or alcohol to relax. You must clean up your mind, clear up your diet and prepare yourself to spend time with God.

It is up to you to decide how you want out of your life. If it depends on you working 60 hours a week, then you need to figure out a better way. If you have children, stop letting strangers raise them. They became your 1st priority when you decided to raise them. You can no longer allow television, advertisers and the government to train your children. Do you really want your children exposed to a life that is based on appearances, possessions and sex? That is what they are being taught. If they can steal the children, then they can win the war for their souls.

You are their moral compass and you need to decide what direction to lead them. If they see their Mother in a number of relationships and their brothers and sisters all have different Fathers, what does that teach them? An absentee

MAY THE SEEDS OF DECEIT BE BLOWN AWAY LIKE CHAFF FROM THE WHEAT

Father can't lead his family. A single Mother can't afford to be a Mom, because she is too busy trying to feed her children.

Today nothing is sacred to the people. Marriage is an afterthought and a disposable inconvenience. The morality of the world is equal to Sodom! There must be a return to the teachings of Christ Jesus. There must be a return to an honorable life.

Know this, everyone will face their lives when you pass into God's realm. How will you explain your actions and your attitude? You need to heed the teachings that are being given in love. You are loved and no one is beyond redemption! All you have to do is humble yourself, see your mistakes and offer it all to Christ. Only this way can you wipe your slate clean. Once God forgives, He forgets your mistakes and from that moment you will be free to start over. You will have to forgive yourself, because guilt will keep you tied to the past

If you are to break free you must speak yourself into your new mindset. You will have watered the seed of God that you were born with. Each day you must water the seed with prayer and

ONE LIFE...ONE LOVE...ETERNAL

MAY THE SEEDS OF DECEIT BE BLOWN AWAY LIKE CHAFF FROM THE WHEAT

gratitude. This will call the living water of Christ. As you practice faith the seed will grow.

This is the parable of the mustard seed. The smallest seed can grow into a mighty tree. Your love is the key to growth, you see Christ is the food that feeds the seed. A plant cannot grow without light and Christ is the Light.

It is time to grow up in faith and start living a true life. Be consistent, be faithful and steadfast! I tell you this, if the mind rebels against this and your friends and family come against this, then the enemy is coming against you. He will use your fear, he will put people against you and he will do everything he can to stop your progress.

Each time you begin to take a new step to a new level of truth, someone will try to stop you. If the voice in your head at 3A.M. tells you to stop, then you are fighting an attack of the enemy. Satan wants to stop you and take you back into the darkness.

Just as you will begin to have dreams and visions, you will have to fight your enemy when he comes against you. The greater the work or the more spiritual the person, the stronger the attack will be. Your weapon against this is Christ Jesus.

ONE LIFE...ONE LOVE...ETERNAL

MAY THE SEEDS OF DECEIT BE BLOWN AWAY LIKE CHAFF FROM THE WHEAT

When the name of the Lord is spoken aloud, Satan and his minions will have to flee. Nothing can stand against the name of the Lord.

>When you struggle…whisper His name
>When you are lost…whisper His name
>When you need strength…whisper His name

There is a power in the spoken word and His name is the most powerful weapon. There is a world of miracles and wonders that await those who choose to accept the calling of the Lord God.

Fame and fortune fades like the setting sun. It might be beautiful for the moment, but the sun will eventually set. Love never dies. Love causes the Angels to weep in joy. Love calls all good into being.

Do you want to hear the Angels sing your praise to God? Do you want to make it to the Kingdom where there is no darkness or turning of shadow? Come and join us and we will rejoice because our prodigal child will be coming home. We will wrap you in a Holy Garment, we will prepare the feast for you and all will sing the songs of God for you. The most beautiful music in Creation will be sung,

ONE LIFE…ONE LOVE…ETERNAL

MAY THE SEEDS OF DECEIT BE BLOWN AWAY LIKE CHAFF FROM THE WHEAT

filled with praise for the lost child that has come home.

The narrow path leads to the banquet, but not all make it. Many are received at the gate and they are greeted by friends and family. There is peace there for them, but they are not allowed into the Kingdom. They are limited to the garden until they progress to the point they can enter.

The people who have near death experiences where they see the Light of God and they see their families, but that is usually as much as they see. They return to body with the vision of the garden and the joy. They try to describe the love you feel everywhere, but that is indescribable. They are given this gift to inspire them to return and finish their work. In God's unending Grace, they have been given another chance.

The same is true for those who see the darkness and others see the fires of Hell. This is their chance to walk away from the life that leads there. You see, God goes to great lengths to reach out to His children. He loves you so much He died for you. Christ shed His Holy Blood on the cross. He suffered the sins of man, so you could have redemption. When He passed on the cross, the skies darkened and the Earth shook. Time

ONE LIFE...ONE LOVE...ETERNAL

MAY THE SEEDS OF DECEIT BE BLOWN AWAY LIKE CHAFF FROM THE WHEAT

stopped, the veil of separation tore and the temple floor broke.

This broke the hold the priests had on the people. They had dishonored their Temple when they plotted and allowed the Man without sin to be persecuted, beaten and hung on the tree of shame. Christ threatened their position and power. I tell you this, they fell on their faces in fear, because they knew what they has done.

We here want you to understand why Christ sacrificed Himself for you. If there had only been you, He would have done this. You are that important to Him!

How important is He to you? What are you willing to do? It's not enough to say the words. It's not enough to believe you are under Grace, so it's going to be alright. It's not enough to say that God is love and He knows I am a good person.

It is enough, if you dedicate yourself to your Creator. It is enough to make a covenant with God to live for Him. The Lord deserves your devotion, He deserves your love and He deserves you to be steadfastly faithful.

We have given you the tools and the knowledge to know the truth. Stand forewarned, once you

MAY THE SEEDS OF DECEIT BE BLOWN AWAY LIKE CHAFF FROM THE WHEAT

know there is no excuse when you approach the throne. God sheds a tear for the child He must turn away. There will come a time when He calls a halt to the workers for the Kingdom. There will be one hand extended to the faithful children and the other hand will hold the sword of judgment. That is the time when, prayers, apologies and tears will fall on deaf ears. There will come a time of separation and the unholy will be cast out.

We here want you to know how much you are loved. We want you to come home to a life of peace that is only found in God. We extend the hand of mercy and love to you. If you will speak to us, we will hear you. If you knock, the door will open to you. Whatever you need to grow in the Kingdom will be given to you.

Love brought this to you.

79 GETTING READY TO STAND

The Lord is with you today. We have written many things about faith, creative powers, staying on path, etc. There comes a time when reading and being taught is not enough.

ONE LIFE....ONE LOVE....ETERNAL

MAY THE SEEDS OF DECEIT BE BLOWN AWAY LIKE CHAFF FROM THE WHEAT

This is the time where you need to put into practice what you have been taught. You have been given the foundation of knowledge, now it is the time to put it together in order to learn to do the Lords work.

You are a creation of God. Regardless what the atheists and the scientists try to prove, you are not an accident! God assembled the universe out of thought, spoke the word and the universe began. Time is of no consequence to God. If God choses, he can move you to a new place or a new time. That which has happened in the world is just one concept. God can change the concept of the world in an instant!

Questioning God is like questioning the air you breathe. It is there and without it, you can't live. God gave you your life, He breathed a spirit into you and that brought life. When the spirit leaves the body, a shell of mere flesh is left behind. The spirit is the core of your existence, so why do you ignore your center, which is your God connection.

This is the foundation of life, but it is ignored and left idle. Picture this when you stand before the mirror, you see your reflection, but imagine you can see the spirit man within. How would he look? Is he strong and fit? Is he glowing with

MAY THE SEEDS OF DECEIT BE BLOWN AWAY LIKE CHAFF FROM THE WHEAT

energy and life? Or do you see a fit healthy body, but does the spirit man look weak and anorexic, like he hasn't been fed or exercised? Is his aura dark and dull, polluted with all the garbage the world has placed on top of him?

Anything that is ignored will diminish and grow ill. You must feed love and nurture anything, if you want it to thrive. Prayer feeds the spirit man, praise draws God's presence and worship draws you into alignment, so the Holy Spirit can clean out the world and feed your inner man.

If you are to do the work of God, you must begin to worship your Creator. Allow God to feed you and heal your spirit. God can take all that damage and make you whole. Don't wait until you are crying out to God at 3AM for help, feeling completely alone, unloved and unwanted, searching for help because your world has fallen apart and you are at rock bottom. There is no reason to wait for the terror in the night to call out to God, for he is with you, right now and He is reaching out to you!

Regardless of the demons you are wrestling with, God is more powerful and He can clean out the lies, the damage and the pain. All you have to do is open your mouth and ask, open your heart and

MAY THE SEEDS OF DECEIT BE BLOWN AWAY LIKE CHAFF FROM THE WHEAT

receive. Pride is the greatest barrier to humbling yourself before God. The Devil tells you that you don' need this, that you can handle it all and you can do whatever you want, because you have free will.

Yes you have free will, that's why

> *You must come before God and ask for help. Whatever has happened to you, know this, God didn't cause it. God gave you the strength to endure and survive. The Lord in all His Mercy and grace is there for the abused, the addicted and the abandoned. Christ Jesus came to show you that even the purest will be abandoned, betrayed and abused. He gave His earthly life to show you that the spirit is eternal, though the body may be destroyed, God gives life.*

How much more can anyone give you, than to be born into a time when man was so lost, the church was corrupt and full of pride? His people were so lost, that God took a part of His Spirit and

MAY THE SEEDS OF DECEIT BE BLOWN AWAY LIKE CHAFF FROM THE WHEAT

came to Earth. Christ showed the world what was possible for each of you to do. He showed us how every one of you could live a life of miracles and healing. When He departed, He provided us with His Holy Spirit so that we could be one with Him for all eternity. Never again would man have to rely on priests to cover your sins for a year. You have been given a direct connection with God. God the Father of us all, Christ Jesus and the Holy Spirit are one entity that works to guide you.

God is tired of wiping your nose, changing your diapers and carrying you around. His children continue to question and keep going over and over the same issues, when they have been taken care of. You keep dragging the same old things off of the Throne and carrying them around.

It is time to start working in harmony with the God force that is implanted in all of God's children. If you are ready to grow up, there is a life of God's works awaiting. A life of love, peace and miracles await all who are willing to do what is necessary to be a God filled person.

You are God's number one priority. We the Guides, Guardians and Teachers, sent forth by God to speak are calling out to you. This is written so you can see the truth! Cast out all of the lies of

ONE LIFE...ONE LOVE...ETERNAL

MAY THE SEEDS OF DECEIT BE BLOWN AWAY LIKE CHAFF FROM THE WHEAT

the world, see the magnificence of a God filled spirit.

Is this too much for you to handle? Is this too much trouble in your busy life? Are you going to continue to be sitting pacified and hypnotized by the world? How much time do you spend starting at an electronic box?

This is a matter of survival! Your time is passing you by! Are you a leader? Are you a healer? Are you a teacher? How will you grasp the reins of your life and fulfill your purpose? Who will take your place if you walk away? Who will touch the life you were meant to save?

Someone is drowning and they won't know how to reach out and take a hand to pull them out to safety. What if it's your hand and your word that they need? God needs you to do His works. He gave this realm to man, all we can do is teach and advise. God can only act through you, His children. If you want to stop the insanity, you are going to have to take a stand. God is calling you and it's time to grow up and recognize the truth. You are not helpless. You can wield the hand of God if you choose to do so. Free will is like the double edged sword of the mouth, it can damage your life and the lives around you.

ONE LIFE...ONE LOVE...ETERNAL

MAY THE SEEDS OF DECEIT BE BLOWN AWAY LIKE CHAFF FROM THE WHEAT

Create a life or throw it all away… the choice lies with the individual.

From now on we will teach how to grow up and walk. Be at peace…you are loved… God is reaching out to you.

ONE LIFE…ONE LOVE…ETERNAL

MAY THE SEEDS OF DECEIT BE BLOWN AWAY LIKE CHAFF FROM THE WHEAT

80 WHY WE MUST STAND

There is an awakening coming to the world. To you the Guides send their love. All of the Universe is in the hands of Almighty God. This is the work of the dedicated, because the love of God dictates this work. You will begin to understand the will of God and you will feel the presence of God. All that matters to us is the work of God. Know God honors His faithful. It is known to us who is steadfast in the Lord.

This is a time of growth and we will speak boldly the truth of the Holy Spirit! Your faith is the cornerstone of your work. This is the foundation for all of the work of God. Our desire is to start a movement that will spread and the fire of the truth will consume the hungry, who are striving to fill the empty void in their life. Know this, you are the called children of God.

Understand these truths and plant them deep into your heart... This life is your training ground. The truth is you serve a supernatural God, the church has diminished the truth so they can have dominion over the people. The truth is you are God's most beloved creation. God made you in

MAY THE SEEDS OF DECEIT BE BLOWN AWAY LIKE CHAFF FROM THE WHEAT

His image, He breathed the soul into you and you were created to work hand in hand with God.

You are not a spiritual orphan that is abandoned to the world, but it is up to you to call upon your spiritual family. God can't be a stranger to you, just as He isn't a vengeful old man sitting on a throne, waiting for you to fall so He can punish.

If you want to know God, then you need to get to know Him through Christ. God came to the world so you could get to know the truth! Most of what God taught through the physical manifestation of Christ has been lost due to the interference of man. Mankind cannot see to accept the true nature of God.

The guides, guardians and teachers here do not understand how you can prefer the life that the enemy of man lays before you. Every lie, every temptation and every path the enemy lays before you, is there to separate you from your Creator.

Lucifer is a jealous entity that hates all of mankind! God loved Lucifer, but the jealousy of not being equal to God was more than he could tolerate. Then God created man and told the Hosts that they were to serve mankind, because you are His beloved. Lucifer swore to destroy

ONE LIFE...ONE LOVE...ETERNAL

MAY THE SEEDS OF DECEIT BE BLOWN AWAY LIKE CHAFF FROM THE WHEAT

man. Evicted from paradise, Lucifer was cast out of paradise and He is down upon the Earth today, working against you. Lucifer loves to destroy the life of man, to show God how weak and pathetic His special children are.

All that you are is dependent on your understanding of the war that is being waged for your life. If you choose the way of Lucifer, you will reside with the one that hates you.

The only protection for you and the ones you love is in the arms of God. Which one you choose is up to you. In Lucifer lays a life of strife and destruction. Drugs, alcohol, sexual addictions and the selfishness of the ego, are the tools of your enemy. If you play on his turf, then you will have to live by his rules. You will find no grace or mercy at his feet.

The Lord of all wants you to live a life of joy and love. Live at peace in the love of God.

> *Acts 26:18 open their eyes, and to turn them from darkness to light, and from the power of Satan and unto God, that they may receive forgiveness of sins, and the inheritance among them*

ONE LIFE...ONE LOVE...ETERNAL

MAY THE SEEDS OF DECEIT BE BLOWN AWAY LIKE CHAFF FROM THE WHEAT

which are sanctified by the faith that is in Christ.

ONE LIFE...ONE LOVE...ETERNAL

www.ingramcontent.com/pod-product-compliance
Lightning Source LLC
Chambersburg PA
CBHW051647040426
42446CB00009B/1018